Praise for *Blood Spatter* (forensics for fiction)

"Writers, you must buy Geoff Symon's nonfiction book *Blood Spatter*! Deliciously gory and ghoulishly fun to read."
– Kristan Higgins, *New York Times*, *USA TODAY*, *Wall Street Journal*, and *Publishers Weekly* bestselling author

"Writer friends! Did you see that Geoff Symon's *Blood Spatter (forensics for fiction)* is now out??? Geoff is such an incredible resource!"
– Laura Kaye, *New York Times* and *USA TODAY* bestselling author

"*Blood Spatter (forensics for fiction)* should be front and center in every suspense writer's resource library. Run, don't walk. You need this book!"
– Kimberly Kincaid, *USA Today* bestselling author

"Only Geoff Symon could make blood spatter so damned charming!"
– Amy Lane, award-winning, bestselling author

Blood Spatter

Forensics for Fiction Series

by Geoff Symon

Blood Spatter (Forensics for Fiction series) by Geoff Symon.
Copyright © 2016 Evil Mastermind, LLC. Manufactured in the United States of America. All rights reserved. No part of this publication may be reproduced, distributed or transmitted in any form or by any electronic or mechanical means including information storage and retrieval systems without permission in writing from the publisher, except by a reviewer, who may quote brief passages in a review.

Published by Evil Mastermind, LLC
New York, NY
www.EvilMastermind.com

First Publication: 15 August 2016

Edited by Tere Michaels
Illustrations by Evil Mastermind, LLC
Book formatting by BB eBooks

ISBN 978-1-945043-10-9 (Ebook)
ISBN 978-1-945043-11-6 (Print)

Website: www.ForensicsForFiction.com

⚥ Copyright © 2016 by Evil Mastermind, LLC, All Rights Reserved

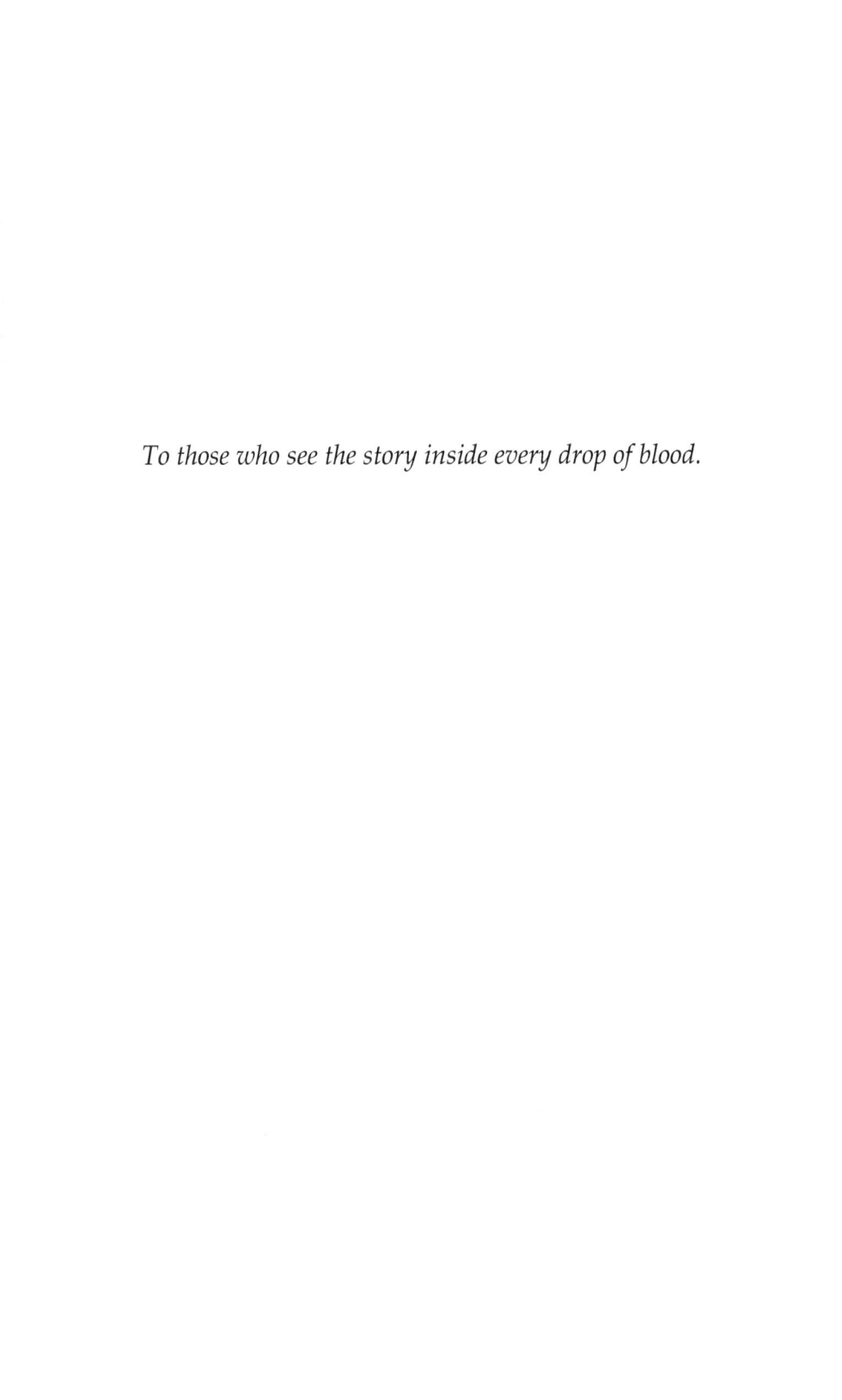

To those who see the story inside every drop of blood.

Contents

Acknowledgements	ix
Preface	xi
Chapter 1: Introduction	**1**
Some Basics	3
History Of Blood Spatter Analysis	5
Chapter 2: Blood Characteristics	**9**
Physics Of Liquids	12
Bloodstain Characteristics	15
Case Study #1:	
Curtis Pope – A Drip is All It Takes	**27**
Chapter 3: Types of Patterns	**35**
Spatter Stains	35
Impact Patterns	36
Cast-Off Patterns	41
Other Patterns	47
Altered Stains	50
Passive Stains	56
Miscellaneous Stains	60

Chapter 4: Processing the Scene   63
  Bloodstain Pattern Analysts   63
  Processing Bloodstains   66
    Preparation   66
    Considering The Big Picture   68
    Documentation   69
    Pattern Assessment   72
    Crime Reconstruction   82
    Outdoor Scenes   89

Exercise: Shower Spatter   95

Case Study #2:
Bret Harris – The Blood Doesn't Lie   101

Chapter 5: Writing Your Scene   109
  Spatter Menu   112
  Writing Examples   122
  Spatter Chart   131
  Closing Thoughts   133

Glossary   135
Bibliography   147
Index   149
About the Author   153

Acknowledgements

So many people were involved with getting the blood of this project flowing. Many thanks to Pamela Burford, Kimberly Kincaid, Jillian Stein, and Thomas DeWitt for their enthusiasm, advice, time and support.

Unequalled thanks goes to Tere Michaels, who converted passionate babble into compelling words.

And thank you to my partner in crime, who bleeds inspiration, and is the reason why this book exists.

Preface

When I taught forensics studies at the George Washington University in Washington, DC, and Marymount University in Maryland, I was amazed at my dedicated and enthusiastic students. As an adjunct professor, I first fully grasped how much interest exists for a career field to which I've dedicated twenty years.

I live with a successful author. Three years ago various writing groups and conventions began inviting me to present forensic courses at their gatherings. Authors turned out to be even hungrier for realism than I'd expected. They might deal in make-believe, but they wanted their stories anchored in truth.

All the different writer audiences made one thing clear: few reference books hit the sweet spot between minutiae and fluff. While many books exist on crimes and investigative techniques, very few address the unique challenges of writing genre fiction.

That need gave birth to the *Forensics for Fiction Series*. In these books, I'm distilling all of my training and experience as a twenty-year forensic investigator and my personal involvement with the genre community. Each book will provide a targeted overview of a different aspect of criminal investigations. I'll present each topic as a heaping platter of research goodies for writers of every genre to choose from, depending on what works for the story in front of them.

I want this book to be accessible and helpful, so rather than bury you under a wall of impenetrable text, I've broken up each chapter with insets:

- *PROCEDURES* and *TERMS*: highlighting how real-life law enforcement officials operate and actual language they use.
- *ACCURACY* and *PITFALLS*: providing practical tips to steer authors away from common errors.
- *FUN FACTS*: sharing entertaining tidbits to spark an idea or inspire a plot bunny
- *ALERTS*: identifying specialized sections that may only interest exhaustive researchers. Whenever you see the Alert symbol—

—I am letting you know that the following section may be more technical than your book requires. If you don't need to know the physics and math involved, feel free to skip these marked sections. You can pick up at the next section seamlessly.

I make sure to provide plenty of illustrations to clarify and drive home every concept. Additionally, I include true-crime case studies relevant to the topic and talk about my own investigations.

I hope you find this book informative and entertaining, but mostly hope you find it useful in your next great story.

Chapter 1: Introduction

"The blood is the life."
Dracula by Bram Stoker

If Renfield's assertion of blood is accurate, is it any wonder that authors use it all the time in their work? Blood boils, its pressure rises, it swells, it flows. There are blood oaths and bloodlines, and don't even get me started on blood lusts. There are blood brothers, which are different from blood relatives. The Bloods and the Crips fueled their blood rage for decades. A blood sausage can share a menu with a blood orange. And I'm certain, somewhere out there, someone has written the story of a bloodhound searching for the Blood Diamond under a Blood Moon. If blood is indeed life, then it pulses through the pages of every genre.

Blood Spatter: Forensics for Fiction Series aims to help writers in all categories of fiction understand blood itself, particularly as it appears in a crime scene and the way it contributes to case resolution. However, even if your story is not focused on an investigation, I hope to convey how blood acts in environments outside the body so that if you use it to any degree, your description is realistic.

Some of the analysis of blood can come across as quite technical, and some math equations will be touched upon, but fear not, Gallant Author, I promise to keep this material accessible, even to the most cursory of skimmers.

Many people equate the topic of blood to gore, and while there are crime scenes involving dismemberment or other horror-script-worthy atrocities, blood is also involved in many everyday situations that are neither disturbing nor repulsive. I would argue that most parents have abundant experience bandaging a scrape or cut for their little ones. They aren't grossed out by it, because dealing with blood is part of life. You see, the properties of blood that cause it to act in predictable ways hold true to the drip from a paper cut as much as they do to stories that involve chainsaws. And Texans.

Crime, and therefore blood, can exist in every genre of fiction, and my goal is to provide the fundamental understanding of what I've learned and experienced in my investigative career to bring a sense of realism to your stories. So let's bloody well get started!

Humans are hardwired to pay attention to the red stuff. Its very presence can indicate danger, mortality or someone in need of aid. When writing, adding blood to an incident heightens the severity of the crime depicted in the scene. Blood conveys violence, malice, and injury, increasing drama and suspense in any context. While some audiences may turn away at the sight of blood, investigators (and some writers!) gravitate towards it. Blood provides invaluable evidence in crime reconstructing and the identification of those involved. Blood can be a source of copious information for the investigator, revealing the sort of injuries sustained, pinpointing the location of where the injury occurred, or highlighting any indication of evidence tampering or body relocation. Blood reveals this by its presence as well as its absence, by how much or little remains, by the individual shapes it forms and by the overall patterns it makes. This crime scene discipline is called a **Blood Spatter Analysis**.

> TERMS – Blood Spatter Analysis, also known as Bloodstain Pattern Analysis, is the systematic process of interpreting bloodstain patterns to reconstruct the crime.

Some Basics

The earliest lesson anyone writing about crime scene investigations should learn is the proper nomenclature. Notice the spelling: blood *SPATTER* analysis, not *SPLATTER*. These words sound the same and in most cases they can be used interchangeably. But if an author wants to add credibility to the story in the context of blood, the official crime scene procedure is called blood *spatter* analysis throughout every law enforcement community. Saying "blood *splatter* analysis" will telegraph a lack of research or attention to detail.

> ACCURACY – It's spatter, not splatter.

The first step in understanding bloodstain pattern analysis is to understand what makes up blood spatter. **Blood spatter**, essentially, is an overall pattern caused by the arrangement of many individual bloodstains. The important thing to remember is investigators never make the analysis off of a single blood drop stain, but instead off of all of the stains together in the pattern. Most stains are made by blood drops, also referred to as droplets. Each stain varies in shape and size depending on several factors, including:

- The force used to create the blood drop.
- The direction the blood drop was flung off in.
- The angle at which it struck the surface.
- The type of surface it impacted.

You'll learn how all of these affect the resulting pattern in the coming chapters, but first let's do a quick history of bloodstain pattern analysis as an investigative tool.

> **ACCURACY** – A bloodstain can be infinitesimally tiny, made by the smallest of blood drops or as large as a pool of blood in the middle of the floor.

History Of Blood Spatter Analysis

Although records of interpreting bloodstain patterns exist throughout history, it is Dr. Paul Leland Kirk who gets credited for the systematic procedure of analyzing blood spatter at crime scenes. He devoted an entire chapter to the subject in his book *Crime Investigation* (1953). As a result, in 1954, he applied his blood spatter analysis as a criminalist in the Sam Sheppard case. Sheppard was a successful neurosurgeon from Ohio who was found guilty of killing his pregnant wife and sent to jail. The high profile case prompted such an extreme media frenzy that the Supreme Court ruled there was enough of a "carnival atmosphere" to consider the original trial tainted. They ordered Sheppard released to await a retrial. Kirk was called in after the fact, and based upon his analysis of blood trails, void patterns and the way blood was patterned on Sheppard's watch, concluded Sheppard could not have been the murderer. During the retrial, Kirk's testimony was relied upon heavily by the defense. The conviction was overturned and Sheppard was acquitted.

> FUN FACT – The Sam Sheppard case gained such notoriety a fictional account was written as the television show and movie we know as *The Fugitive*.

Herbert MacDonell was the next person to significantly study crime reconstruction from bloodstains. MacDonell conducted methodical experimentation under which he would create the stain patterns to study. From hitting blood-filled sponges with baseball bats to shooting pigs' heads he obtained from the butcher, MacDonell was able to scientifically show what sort of patterns resulted from specific stimuli. He first reported his findings in his *Flight Characteristics and Stain Patterns of Human Blood* (1971).

MacDonell later established the Bloodstain Evidence Institute in Corning, NY. His studies were recognized by the International Association for Identification and led to his participation in many high profile cases, including the O.J. Simpson murder trial.

Other high-profile consultants such as Tom Bevel, Stuart James, Paul Kish and Henry Lee have all furthered the study of blood spatter analysis and applied the principles to hundreds of cases. Their interpretation of blood made recreating what happened at each scene possible. These essential principles can answer so many questions for the investigators:

- What type of injury occurred (gunshot vs beating, for example)?
- How many injuries were there?
- Where exactly in the room did the blood-inducing wound(s) happen?
- What sort of movement happened inside the scene?
- Is anything missing from the scene?
- Was the body moved?
- Are there blood impressions to help identify the suspect?
- Does the blood match the suspect's story?

> **ACCURACY** – Keep in mind that a single small stain does not create a spatter pattern.

We will explore how blood tells all of these tales as the book progresses. But first, it is important to learn the make-up of blood itself so you can anticipate how it will act when present at a scene. So, next chapter we'll begin with the intrinsic characteristics of blood.

Chapter 2: Blood Characteristics

Any lesson on blood spatter should start with the physical properties of blood. Without an understanding of how blood acts in specific situations, writers cannot guarantee any sort of realism in their fictional bloodstain patterns.

Think of it this way: For readers to accept "Tammy" as a believable character in your latest story, you have to establish her personality, her motivations, what makes her tick. Her actions and reactions must ring true to the person you've created.

The very same goes for this topic; how authentic is the blood you're writing? Like "Tammy," blood has its own patterns of behavior based on the circumstances affecting it. Does your use of fictional blood reflect its real life properties and established traits? Whether writer or investigator, in order to identify and interpret different bloodstain patterns, you first must understand the characteristics of blood.

As a liquid, blood reacts to forces and environments just as other fluids do. In physics, we use concepts such as viscosity (a liquid's thickness) and surface tension (what holds a liquid together) to explain how the liquid acts, be it blood, water or tequila. In this way, thinking of our everyday experiences helps tremendously in deciphering how blood in a crime scene created the patterns left behind. This question, at its most basic, underpins the concept of blood spatter analysis: what must have happened previously to create the patterns we see now?

> **ACCURACY – All liquids follow the laws of physics, including blood.**

What happens to the lower cabinets and kitchen floor when your child drops the carton of milk? Why does the honey left on the teaspoon drip to the counter? Where does water spray on the bathroom walls if you run the shower without closing the curtain?

Our daily lives provide ample experience in which we can see how a liquid reacts to different forces. When that carton hits the floor, the milk erupts in every direction, splashing onto the refrigerator, spraying across the cabinets, pooling on the floor. We can clearly visualize the disaster happening, from slippery fingers to milky mess. A spatter analysis employs the same visual, just viewed in reverse.

As identified in the above examples, liquids travel through the air, carried by a force until they hit a surface. It's important to be clear about what the liquid is called at the beginning, middle and end of this action.

For the purposes of this book, we'll refer to the main liquid prior to any sort of force being applied as the **parent**, which would be the milk in the carton, the honey on the spoon and the water prior to exiting the shower head. For blood it's the blood inside the person prior to injury.

Once the parent ejects the liquid, I refer to the individual orbs in the air as **drops** or **droplets**.

Once the droplet hits the floor, wall, ceiling or other surface and settles into its final shape, that is called the **stain**.

A blood drop and bloodstain are the same blood, just at different points on its journey. For blood spatter analysis, the investigators must interpret the bloodstains, which are the end of the blood's voyage, and that's why the analysis occurs backwards.

> FUN FACT – Each body only gives you about a gallon of blood to play with; and that's only if it's completely drained.

A normal healthy adult has approximately 4.5 to 6.0 liters of blood (*Human Anatomy* (5th Edition) Jan 12 2016 by Kenneth Saladin), which is approximately 1.0 to 1.5 gallons. Think about a gallon of milk, like the one the child dropped in the above example. That's pretty analogous to the amount of blood we each have in our bodies.

Very rarely do you find that much blood at a crime scene, and if you do, no credible investigator would assume the victim was completely drained. Logic leaps like this can wreck an investigation – or book. In that instance, the more likely answer is there is more than one victim. Conversely, also be aware that if you're writing a bloody scene that only involves one intended target, you cannot have your investigators conclude there were three gallons of blood present.

Physics Of Liquids

Once you've decided how bloody your fictional scene is going to be, you need to know how that blood reacted to the force that caused the injury. The two properties of liquids that come into play are *viscosity* and *surface tension*.

> TERMS – Viscosity is a liquid's resistance to flow; its thickness.

Blood's **viscosity** is slightly higher than water's, meaning blood is quite literally thicker than water. For an extreme comparison, honey has a much greater viscosity than blood or water. In general terms, whole milk has a closer viscosity to blood than water does, so if you can imagine how whole milk flows as compared to how water does, you have a good approximation to how blood would compare to water.

> TERMS – Surface tension is the internal force within a liquid that keeps the liquid together.

Surface tension is what keeps a liquid together, therefore a force must be applied to separate a liquid (drop/drip/etc.) from its parent pool.

Think of splashing in a bathtub or swimming pool. When you slap the surface of the water, you are adding a force which is sufficient to overcome the water's surface tension and thereby you separate part of the liquid from its parent – you create a splash. If there is not enough force to overcome the surface tension, there is no separation, no splash. So, if you gently put your hand into the water, it simply enters, without separating any water.

When a drip falls from a faucet, gravity is the force that breaks the surface tension. The drip grows until it becomes big enough – heavy enough – for the force of gravity to overcome the water's surface tension.

> TERMS – Gravity is called a *Passive Force* because it is applied naturally without any human involvement.

A drip caused by gravity will always be the standard size drip for that liquid. Gravity is a constant, ever present force on that liquid, so the weight required to overcome the surface tension will always be the same. That weight for the given liquid is always achieved in a specific sized drop. So, for any given liquid, a **passive drip** will create equal-sized drops. The size of the drop varies from liquid to liquid (water to honey to blood), but the size will always be the same for the same liquid (comparing milk to milk or blood to blood). The greater the force used to break the surface tension, the smaller the droplets, which becomes important when doing the backwards analysis.

Surface tension also comes into play when a droplet travels through the air. When we think of raindrops, we typically think of them in a "teardrop" shape. Artists use the teardrop form to indicate movement in a piece of art. In reality, however, droplets are completely spherical. The liquid's surface tension pulls on the exterior of the liquid equally on all sides, holding that liquid together. As a result, the droplet is a perfect sphere. So every raindrop, faucet drip and drop of honey really is just a liquid marble falling to the ground. Knowing that bloodstain shapes and sizes were created by *spherical* blood drops helps to recreate how that end pattern was made.

Figure 1: The teardrop shape artists use for falling liquids

Figure 2: The actual, spherical shape of a falling drop

Bloodstain Characteristics

The shape of a bloodstain is the first indication of what may have happened. Its shape reveals the direction the blood was traveling. Investigators use this directionality to determine the location and body position of the people involved.

Of course, many factors helped to create the bloodstain's shape. Was the droplet traveling through the scene or was it in free fall? What was the size of the droplet? What type of surface did it land on? Investigators must consider all of these elements to interpret blood spatter accurately.

> TERMS – Trajectory is the path a blood drop took from the point of injury to the stain on a surface. A "free fall" trajectory refers to a passive drip falling straight down due to gravity. Any other path requires a force greater than gravity to carry the drop through the scene, away from the straight down route.

The angle of the blood drop's impact to the surface relates directly to the shape of the resulting stain. Keep in mind the word "surface" refers not only to the ground, but to any surface impacted. This can be horizontal, such as the floor or ceiling, vertical, such as a wall, or anything in between.

When blood falls straight down and hits a smooth, hard, nonporous surface (like bathroom tile) at 90 degrees, it creates a circular stain. Any trajectory that is not at a 90-degree impact, even if only slightly off, creates an elongated stain. The following chart shows what each stain looks like at angles 10 degrees apart from each other, where 90 degrees represents free fall and 10 degrees is the droplet traveling almost parallel to the ground, wall or other surface.

| 90° | 80° | 70° | 60° | 50° | 40° | 30° | 20° | 10° |

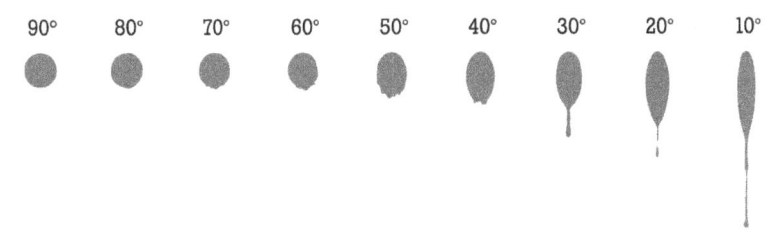

Figure 3: Bloodstain shapes at different angles of impact

> **PROCEDURE – Stain Shape –** Circular stains are created by perpendicular (90 degree) impacts. The smaller the impact angle, the more elongated the resulting stain.

Most blood drop stains in a violent scene will be oval because the force involved – which is greater than gravity – carried the droplet through the scene. So, why does the droplet create an oval?

In your mind, visualize the blood drop sphere, or "marble," traveling almost parallel to the ground. When the droplet gets to the point of initial contact with the ground, it's going to start leaving a mark, but the mark is not going to be very big because it's barely touching. As the droplet continues moving, gravity is still pulling it down, so it connects more and more with the ground, leaving more blood behind and widening the stain until the stain is as wide as the droplet sphere itself.

Because the drop loses its blood as it "paints" the bloodstain onto the surface, the sphere becomes smaller and smaller. So, once the stain reaches the width of the blood drop, the width begins to decrease again as the droplet shrinks. The width of the stain continues to narrow until there is simply no blood left to leave behind and the droplet is completely gone. The resulting stain is the elongated oval shape.

Elongation

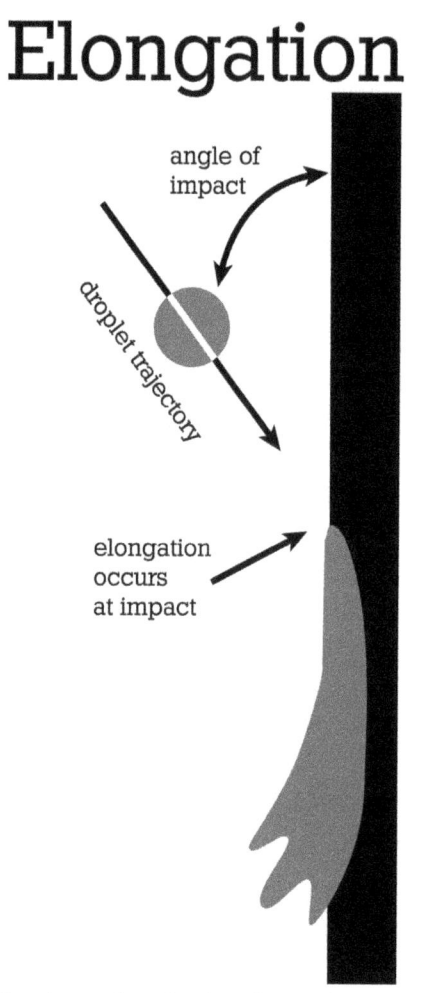

Figure 4: The elongation of a drop from sphere to oval stain

As stated above, the angle at which the droplet hits the surface will determine how elongated the resulting oval stain will be. The greater the impact angle, which means the more the droplet approaches a straight-down fall (or perpendicular strike against a wall), the less elongated the oval stain, until it is purely circular at 90 degrees.

If this seems at all confusing, all you need to remember is two concepts: A straight-down passive drop creates a *circular* stain, and the more a drip which is flung into the room approaches a parallel course with the ground, the *longer* the resulting oval stain will be.

In stains of 30 degrees or less, you'll notice an additional mark extending beyond the stain itself, sort of like an elephant's trunk. This extension is called the **spine** and is known as a cast-off mark, created when the droplet hits the surface.

Figure 5: A spine is the "elephant's trunk" of a stain and points in the direction the stain was traveling

We won't get too much into Newton's Law or any other physics here, but essentially the force required to create these impact angles causes an equal and opposing force when the drop hits the surface. This opposing force is great enough to create a splash that throws out a smaller blood drop ahead of the stain. For all bloodstain pattern analysis, the spine is not considered in any mathematical calculations (addressed in Chapter 4). For that type of analysis, we just use the main drop's ellipse (oval) stain.

The only thing the spine is considered for is to determine which direction the droplet was traveling. Whenever any type of spine is identified in a blood spatter stain, it is always located on the forward side of the stain, because it was thrown ahead of it. In other words, it points in the direction the blood droplet was traveling. So, if we're trying to determine where in the room the victim was hit, we know the blow that caused this particular stain had to have occurred in the opposite direction. This is sometimes confusing to grasp because, as previously stated, drops of water are incorrectly depicted as teardrops, and in a teardrop the "point" is behind the drop, in the direction it originated. In bloodstain pattern analysis, the "point" is in front of the drop.

Another way to determine directionality in a bloodstain is identifying where most of the blood pooled *within* the stain. The force carrying the droplet will keep pushing the blood within the stain in the same direction. So the liquid blood on the surface will be gathered towards the direction the stain was traveling. If you refer back to the different angle of impact stains above, you'll see a jagged edge on the stains from 80 degrees through 40 degrees. This is a result of the blood being forced there. Just like with the spine, the location of the injury is in the opposite direction.

> PROCEDURE – Directionality – Determining what direction the blood was heading also tells you the direction it came from.

These quick determinations of directionality can be very helpful if you want to very broadly test a suspect's story of what happened. However, knowing the direction the stain came from only provides a very general idea of where the injury occurred. Most investigators need a much more specific point of injury – which includes not only exactly how far into the room the blood originated from, but also how high off the ground it was. This way the investigator can actually position the body of the victim, which aids immensely in the crime reconstruction.

We will get into this pinpoint location in much greater depth when we discuss actually processing a scene (Chapter 4), but put broadly, you can apply math to the length and width of a bloodstain to determine the exact angle of impact. If you use that angle at the base of the stain, you can draw a line from the impact site back and up into the room. We then know the blood droplet that created that stain traveled on that line. Therefore, we know the injury occurred somewhere on that line.

Excited yet? We'll revisit this in gory detail in Chapter 4.

Sometimes when a blood drop hits the ground straight down, the tiniest of blood dots result around the main circular stain. These dots are called **satellite** cast-off marks. We already discussed another type of cast-off mark, spines, when we were talking about the directionality of the blood drop. Just as in that situation, these satellite cast-off marks are not considered at all in any calculations. They are the result of the type of surface the blood hit, and have no bearing on any directionality assessment.

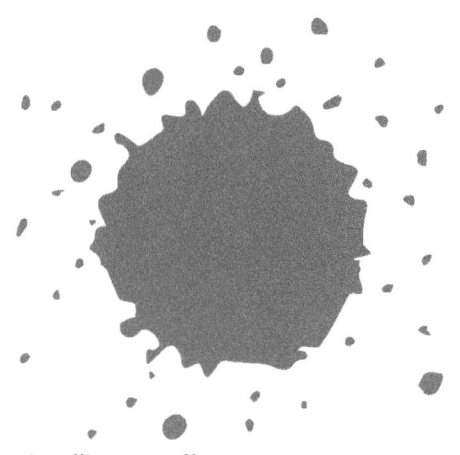

Figure 6: Satellite cast-off stains surround the parent stain

Even at terminal velocity (discussed below), if the blood droplet falls on a smooth, hard, nonporous surface, such as polished metal, glass or ceramic tile, the resulting stain will remain intact with no satellite cast-offs thrown around it. The satellite cast-off spatter generally occurs if the surface is rough or porous, such as on concrete, wood or paper, or if the blood is dripping into blood already on the floor. Satellite cast-offs will be addressed in greater depth in the next chapter.

> PROCEDURE – Spines and Satellites are cast-off marks that are a result of impact and are not considered for any analysis beyond general directionality.

For those disappointed there wasn't enough physics, I have some bonus topics for you below. However, if being overly technical is unnecessary for what you're writing, feel free to jump to the next chapter. The info I provide below is merely for my fellow completists out there.

> ALERT – The following section becomes more technical than most writers need for their stories. The physics ahead is provided for those who desire complete research data. Those needing just the essentials can skip ahead to the next chapter.

The size of the stain almost entirely depends upon the size of the blood drop, the passive drip being approximately 0.05 mL and having an approximate 4.56 mm diameter (*Criminalistics: An Introduction to Forensic Science* (10th Edition) Jan 13, 2010 by Richard Saferstein). However, the height from which the droplet falls can also affect the stain's size, to a lesser degree. Basically, the amount of force a drop hits the ground with will affect how big that stain can get. The pull of gravity will continually increase the velocity of a blood drop in free fall until the air resistance acting against the drop equals the gravitational force. Since gravity is no longer the strongest force acting on the droplet, it can no longer cause the blood to go any faster.

At that point, the drop has reached its **terminal velocity**, meaning it's falling as fast as it can and will stay at that speed. From that point on, the bloodstain size it creates will be consistent. The bloodstain size will gradually increase up until that point. Saferstein documented that blood drops of 0.05 mL created bloodstains with diameters climbing from 13 to 21.5 mm when dropped from heights going from 6 inches up to 7 feet. After 7 feet the diameters remained at 21.5 mm, indicating from that height terminal velocity has been achieved.

Surface tension remains at work even after the blood droplet has created the stain. A liquid's surface tension is always attempting to pull the liquid together; to recreate the sphere. So, once a free falling droplet has hit the ground and created a circular stain, most of the blood in that stain can be found in its center. The surface tension is pulling as much blood together as it can.

If you were to put your eye down to ground level and look at the stain from its side, instead of seeing a flat stain, you would actually see a dome. That's the surface tension in operation. As a result, the center of the stain is the thickest and takes the longest to dry. The outer edges of bloodstains will always dry first.

With these properties of blood in your pocket, you are now ready to get into the patterns themselves. So, next chapter we will jump into actual blood spatter and how crimes create the different patterns investigators find at a scene.

Case Study #1: Curtis Pope – A Drip is All It Takes

Darrell North was a manager for a development company that built branches of a motel chain in Fort Worth, TX. He was known to be tough at the work site, but was remembered as a fair, likable man.

On February 22, 2000, Darrell did not come home. His wife was worried, especially since it was unlike him not to call if he was to be late. When he still had not shown by 11 PM, his adult son, Mark, went to check for Darrell at his on-site construction office. Mark discovered Darrell's car parked by the trailer. He noted the ground underneath was dry, so concluded it had not been moved at all that rainy evening. The lights in the trailer were on, but Mark found the trailer was locked via the outside padlock, which would indicate Darrell had left for the evening.

Concerned, Mark attempted to see inside the trailer through the windows and the door. He saw his father lying face down on the floor. Darrell had two very deep chopping wounds to the back of his head, and had been stabbed forty-six times.

There was a significant amount of blood in the scene, found in two of the three rooms inside the trailer. A trail of blood led from the body to some filing cabinets, another from the body to the desk. On top of the desk was a machete, which was not uncommon for a construction site as brush often had to be removed. There was no discernible blood on it. Interviews revealed that Darrell kept two machetes on site. The second one could not be found. Near the body was a very bloody and bent hole-punch.

The scene showed no indication this was a robbery. The trailer revealed no signs of forced entry via any of the windows or doors. Darrell's wallet was still in his pocket and nothing appeared rummaged or out of place. With no alternative way to exit the trailer, investigators concluded the assailant took the time to lock it up as he was leaving. With nothing apparently stolen, the care to lock up, and the excessive amount of wounds on Darrell's body, investigators believed this was a rage crime with Darrell himself, not the property, as the target.

With so much blood at the scene, it was obvious there had been a struggle. Bloodstain patterns included cast-offs, passive drips, swipes and transfer patterns. Investigators took to the task of seeing what the blood was telling them, not the least of which was movement throughout the scene.

As noted previously, passive drips created at least

two distinct paths through the trailer. Around these paths there appeared to be footprints, indicating either Darrell or his assailant got blood on the bottom of his shoe before walking around the scene.

Crime Scene Investigators use several chemical solutions to improve the clarity of evidence at a scene. For blood, one of these chemical enhancers is Amido Black. This is an amino acid dye that when introduced to certain proteins, like those found in blood, stains the pattern black, making the patterns more visible. After mixing it properly, CSIs spray the Amido Black on a suspected blood pattern.

In this case, after the Amido Black enhancement, investigators were clearly able to see the "Justin" symbol in the enhanced footprints. Justin Boots prints the "Justin" logo on the heel of their boots. Unfortunately, Justin Boots uses the same size heel on different sizes of boots, so determining a foot size from the heel print was not possible. But Darrell was not wearing Justin Boots, so this evidence was still quite significant.

Also found at the scene was a circular bloodstain on Darrell's back left pants leg. The fact that the stain was circular meant it hit at 90 degrees, which indicated it hit the pants leg after Darrell was already lying on the floor. A 90-degree stain is a stain made from a free fall, most often indicating a passive drip from gravity. This means it came from someone standing over Darrell. All of this suggested this stain was created after the violence was over.

The logical conclusion was that whoever was standing over Darrell after he was dead was probably wounded and bleeding. Investigators collected the stain with hopes of finding the assailant's DNA. The assumption that the murderer was bleeding led the investigators to surmise that most of the passive drip stains could be from the attacker, and they collected several of the other 90-degree stains from the floor.

The investigators discovered Darrell sent everyone home early on that day because it had been raining. Darrell had stayed behind because he had a meeting with a swimming pool subcontractor named Curtis Pope. Darrell's wife reported Curtis was a family friend and had worked on their personal pool. She said Darrell had a fondness for Curtis and was trying to help get him back on track after a series of bad choices culminated in him being arrested for petty theft. She said Curtis was always respectful and appreciative towards Darrell.

When interviewed, Curtis acknowledged that he had the meeting with Darrell on that day after everyone else had left. He said the meeting lasted approximately twenty minutes. Curtis said Darrell was still in the trailer when he drove out and had not yet locked up.

The only other probable suspect was a roofing

contractor named Bob Johnson. Darrell had fired Bob two weeks earlier. Bob had no hesitation making his anger with Darrell known. He felt betrayed by Darrell and claimed his firing was unjustified. Just two days after Darrell's murder, Bob called the development company's superintendent and asked for his job back. Bob claimed he was with his child in the hospital on the day of the murder, and although that was verified, the alibi did not cover the entire day.

Based on the blood pattern evidence, police re-interviewed both Curtis and Bob with the intention of taking DNA samples and searching for Justin Boots. Both Curtis and Bob provided their blood and pairs of Justin Boots to the investigators. Bob's boots had a heel that was bigger than the bloodstain. Curtis' boots, however, were the same size as the stain, but they appeared to be brand-new. The interviewers also noted that Curtis had a bruise developing under his left eye, which they had not seen on the day of the murder.

DNA results eventually came back from the blood collected at the scene, and it matched Curtis Pope's DNA. Curtis was arrested and charged with first-degree murder. He posted bail and immediately fled for Canada. Law enforcement caught up with him in Watertown, New York, and brought him back to Texas for his trial, where he was convicted and sentenced to life in prison.

Although only Curtis knows for sure what happened in that trailer, investigators theorize that Darrell had called the meeting with Curtis to fire him for poor work, just as he had done with Bob two weeks earlier. The investigation revealed Curtis was behind on all of his bills and his pool company was on the brink of bankruptcy. Darrell was Curtis' only major employer. Faced with losing his last source of income, Curtis most likely turned the meeting into an argument, which then turned violent.

Investigators believe that Curtis grabbed one of the two machetes Darrell kept in the trailer, while Darrell picked up the hole-punch. Darrell must have gotten in one blow on Curtis' face before Curtis hacked him twice on the back of the head. He then proceeded to stab Darrell forty-six times. The blow to Curtis' face most likely caused a nosebleed, which introduced his blood in the form of passive drips to the scene. The blow also caused him to bruise a few days later.

Police think Curtis left, taking the machete with him and locking up in the misconception that anyone looking for Darrell would think he left. Curtis most likely ditched the clothes he was wearing, including his Justin Boots, and the machete, which would have all been covered in blood. The boots he turned over to the police were brand-new to replace the pair he disposed of.

Blood spatter was significant in this case. It gave investigators leads to follow with the boot prints, but also indicated which blood in this overly bloody scene the investigators should collect for testing. But this entire case really came down to a single drop of blood. There could have been any number of stories, albeit improbable, that Curtis Pope could have come up with to explain why his DNA was mixed up with Darrell North's DNA at the crime scene.

For example, he could have said he got a nose bleed during the meeting and had to leave early to address it. He would then simply claim Darrell was killed by someone else after he was gone. The one drop of blood he would never be able to explain away, however, was that single drip on the back of Darrell's pants leg. The only way that 90-degree drop could have gotten there is if Curtis was standing over Darrell's body after he was dead, making him an obvious participant in this crime.

Chapter 3: Types of Patterns

Now that we've established the basic characteristics of blood, let's discuss the scene it's found in.

What does the blood look like once the investigators arrive? Most blood spatter scenes involve hundreds – if not thousands – of individual bloodstains. However, blood spatter analysis has broken open cases in which there were only a couple of bloodstains, or maybe none at all. Never forget that for some cases, the *absence* of blood can be every bit as significant as scenes where it's present.

The final bloodstains observed are the end result of the violent incident that produced the blood, as well as any activity that changed that original pattern (walking through the blood or trying to wipe it up, for examples) and any gravitational or environmental factors that affected the stains afterward. When discussing bloodstains within a crime scene, they can be mostly grouped into one of three categories: *Spatter Stains*, *Altered Stains* and *Passive Stains*.

Spatter Stains

Spatter Stains themselves indicate violence has

occurred. A force was applied that was able to release individual droplets smaller than those created from gravity. Because the force is greater than gravity, it is able to carry the droplets through the scene. Even if the droplets still land on the floor, they have traveled away from the straight down fall that gravity itself would have caused. Sometimes the force is great enough so that the drops hit a vertical surface, such as a wall or lamp, before they are able to reach the floor. The greater the force applied, the smaller the resulting droplets.

Impact Patterns

Many types of Spatter Stains are **impact patterns**. These are bloodstain patterns that originate from the injury itself. Impact patterns create a random pattern of droplets. Because the pattern is created by the original injury, the random droplets can be used to mathematically determine exactly where they came from, telling us where the blow had to have occurred within the room or environment. This helps in the reconstruction of the crime. We'll discuss the methods used in making that determination, called the Point of Origin, in the next chapter.

The size and distribution of the blood droplets in impact patterns are determined by the amount of force used to cause the injury, and therefore impact patterns are further classified into three subcategories.

CHAPTER 3: TYPES OF PATTERNS

> **PROCEDURE** – Impact spatters are categorized according to their velocity, which is to say how fast the blood was traveling when it hit the surface. The faster the velocity, the greater the force required to create the bloodstain pattern, as well as the smaller the size of the droplets involved.

Low velocity impact spatter stains are stains resulting from a force that is more or less that of gravity. Drips that fall to the floor after an injury are the best example of low velocity impact spatter. Gravity is the key. It is the natural force that overcomes the surface tension and creates the same size drips each time. To make any other size drip requires a force greater than gravity; the greater the force, the smaller the droplet, and any force greater than gravity will result in a stain that is no longer a low velocity impact spatter stain.

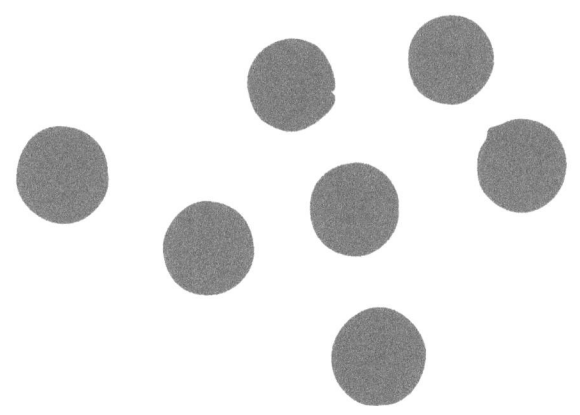

Figure 7: Low velocity impact spatter patterns are individual drips caused by gravity

Some specific examples of low velocity impact spatter that can be used in a fictional crime scene include:

- Blood dripping from the suspect due to an active wound. The passive drips would create a trail behind him as he moved through the scene.
- The blood dripping to the floor from the very bloodied chainsaw used in a very bloody death scene.
- The drips from the shifter's claws after he sliced his prey.
- The victim's blood dripping off the suspect's hand after he attempted to hastily clean up the scene before he fled.

We will discuss many more of these patterns below when we discuss Passive Stains.

Medium velocity impact spatter stains are stains resulting from a force greater than gravity, but generally limited to what a human being can create. Beatings and stabbings most often result in medium velocity impact spatter stains. The individual droplets range in size but are all typically smaller than those created from a low velocity impact.

CHAPTER 3: TYPES OF PATTERNS

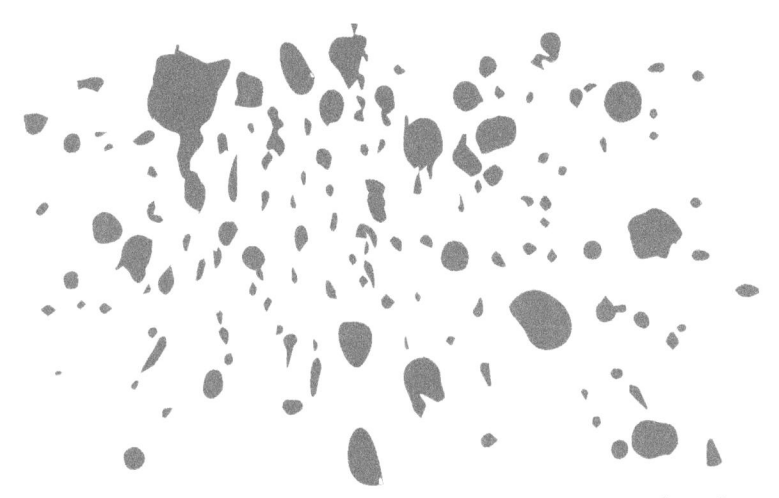

Figure 8: Medium velocity impact spatter patterns consists of smaller stains than gravitational drips

Some situational considerations that result in medium velocity impact spatter include:

- Droplets flung off from a weapon used in a beating, such as a bat or club.
- Droplets thrown from the slashing motion of a knife.
- Blood thrown from the chain of a running chainsaw.
- Blood sprayed when punching someone in the mouth.

High velocity impact spatter stains are stains from an extreme force and are almost exclusively from gunshot wounds. Explosions and some high-speed machinery injuries can also create this spatter pattern. The droplets in these circumstances are incredibly tiny and create a "misting" look in the resulting stain.

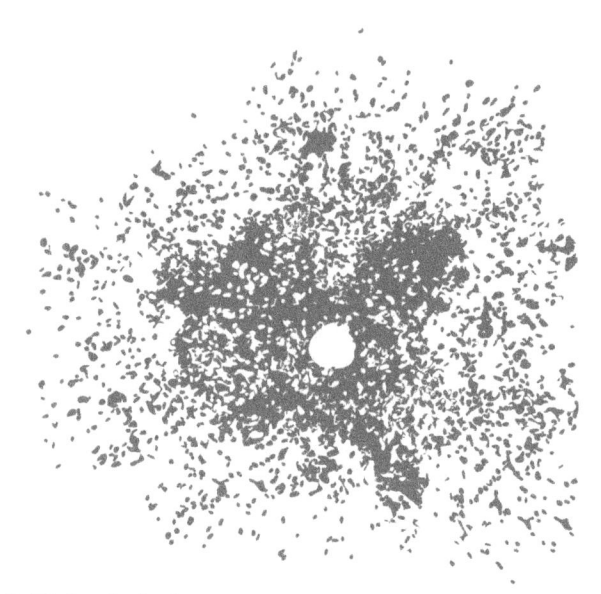

Figure 9: High velocity impact spatter patterns are made up of droplets so small they resemble a mist

While the medium velocity impact from a blunt object creates one wound at the site of the blow, a high velocity impact typically creates two injury sites: the entrance wound and the exit wound. As a result, these types of Spatter Stains are seen both in front of and behind the victim. The entrance wound creates a stain referred to as **back spatter** and, if close enough (typically no farther than four feet), can be found on the weapon and hand of the shooter. The exit wound creates **forward spatter**, and is the misting effect seen above.

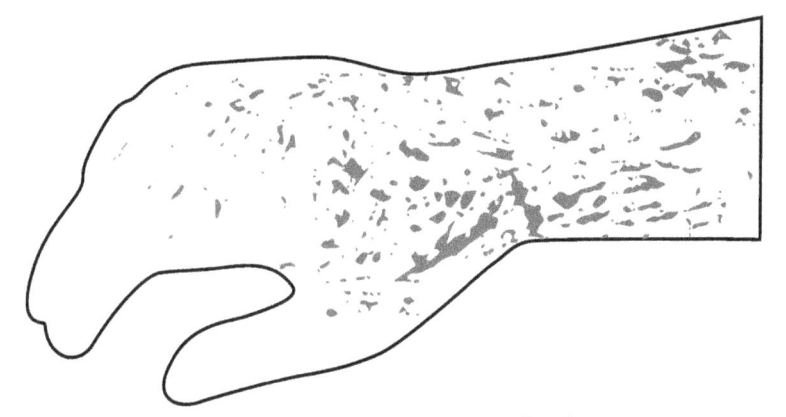

Figure 10: Back spatter can get on the shooter

When writing a story, you have to create an incredibly powerful force to produce high velocity impact spatter. In the real world only a few situations apply:

- The misting blood from a gunshot wound.
- The misting blood from injuries caused in an explosion.
- Any injury from technical equipment/machinery that produces enough force to cause a misting bloodstain.

Cast-Off Patterns

Cast-off patterns are Spatter Stains categorized differently from impact patterns because in cast-off patterns the blood was not projected from the injury site. Instead, these patterns are a result of blood thrown from a bloody object. While impact patterns result from the force causing the injury, cast-off patterns are created from different forces after the injury has occurred.

Before we get into those forces, let's address what many of you are thinking – we already discussed two other stains called cast-off marks in the previous chapter. Neither of those fall into this Spatter Stains category. The first was the splash thrown ahead of a stain, called a spine, caused when a droplet hits a surface at certain angles. The second was a satellite pattern around circular stains created when blood bounces back after hitting the floor.

All of these are called cast-offs because the concept of their creation is the same – smaller drops are *cast off* from a bigger drop/blood source as the result of a different force being applied. The force in these two cast-off marks was the force of hitting the surface.

The cast-off patterns we're going to discuss in this chapter are not from an environmental force, but rather a violent force applied by another person. For that reason these cast-offs are distinct from the previous two, and are included in this Spatter Stains category.

> **TERMS** – Tricky terminology – There are two types of stain categories referred to as "cast-offs." One consists of spines and satellite stains (discussed in Chapter 2). These cast-off marks are created by the impact force and are not considered in any blood spatter analysis. The other cast-off patterns are Spatter Stains created by blood flung off of a bloody weapon or other object. These patterns give significant information aiding in the crime reconstruction.

There are two forces at work when considering Spatter Stain cast-off patterns; *centrifugal force* and *inertia*.

Centrifugal force is the force caused and experienced in a rotational, or arcing, motion. Have you ever been on that carnival ride that places your back against the inner wall of a large circular chamber? The ride was originally known as the *Rotor*, and an updated version is called the *Gravitron*. As the ride begins spinning, it eventually removes the floor from your feet. It's intended to be scary (and it is!) because essentially you are unable to move, and your back is stuck against the wall. What you're experiencing during that ride is the centrifugal force holding you in place.

This same force is at work when someone swings a bloody object. If the centrifugal force of the arcing movement is great enough to exceed the surface tension of the blood, the action will cast off (hence the name) droplets of blood, creating a spatter pattern. The centrifugal force of the incident is directly related to the motion, so the cast-off pattern stain will be a series of droplets lined up in the direction of the motion.

Figure 11: Cast-off pattern line

The other force that causes cast-off patterns is **inertia**. This is the law of physics wherein objects at rest tend to stay at rest, and conversely, objects in motion tend to stay in motion.

What do we all do when mashed potatoes are on the table for dinner? We take up the serving spoon, scoop up a hefty portion and go through the process of trying to get every last bit of that goodness from spoon to plate. Invariably, we end up sharply flicking the spoon repeatedly in an attempt to release the remaining stubborn potatoes clinging to the inside of the spoon. When you do this, you are expressing your expertise in the concept of inertia.

The flicking gesture introduces motion to the potatoes that we abruptly remove when we stop the spoon at the end of the flick. Inertial forces are still at work on the potatoes, pulling them down although the spoon has stopped. If this inertial force is greater than the stickiness that clings the potatoes to the spoon, the potatoes will continue their motion and leave the spoon. The same force works when blood is on something moving.

If the bloody object is in motion and abruptly stops, the blood on that object will want to stay in motion. If that inertial force is greater than the surface tension of the blood, droplets will be *cast off* and make a spatter pattern. This pattern won't follow a nice line like the centrifugal arc patterns, but instead covers an area.

Figure 12: Inertial spatter pattern

I think the best way to bring home the forces at work for these types of patterns is to recall some of the adventure television series of yesteryear. Who would have thought that *Murder, She Wrote*; *Magnum, P.I.*; or *Hart to Hart* would have proved instructive in a blood spatter book? In many of those "gentle" adventure stories, invariably some crook would jump onto the hood of a moving car for some inexpensive stunt work. What would the driver do in this not-as-rare-as-you'd-think occurrence? Either swerve the car all over the road or speed up, then slam on the brakes. Our hood surfer experiences both forces here: swerving left to right and back again creates a centrifugal force, which can throw the crook off the side of the hood. Also, by speeding up and then abruptly stopping, inertia casts the offender forward, off the hood.

Now imagine the thrown man as blood and the car as a bloody hand, baseball bat, or other object, and you have a clear analogy of the creation of cast-off bloodstain patterns.

Let's bring these concepts back to a bloody crime. When a bludgeon weapon is used to beat a victim, that weapon has to be swung in an arc to do the damage. As it's swung back and again when brought forward, centrifugal force is at work pulling the blood off of it along the route. These drops create a line corresponding with the arc's path.

At the end of the back swing, the weapon stops suddenly before starting the forward swing to hit the victim. Inertia is at play at this point, the sudden stop pulling more blood droplets off. Every new swing in the beating creates a new line of centrifugal cast-offs

spoon, the potatoes will continue their motion and leave the spoon. The same force works when blood is on something moving.

If the bloody object is in motion and abruptly stops, the blood on that object will want to stay in motion. If that inertial force is greater than the surface tension of the blood, droplets will be *cast off* and make a spatter pattern. This pattern won't follow a nice line like the centrifugal arc patterns, but instead covers an area.

Figure 12: Inertial spatter pattern

I think the best way to bring home the forces at work for these types of patterns is to recall some of the adventure television series of yesteryear. Who would have thought that *Murder, She Wrote*; *Magnum, P.I.*; or *Hart to Hart* would have proved instructive in a blood spatter book? In many of those "gentle" adventure stories, invariably some crook would jump onto the hood of a moving car for some inexpensive stunt work. What would the driver do in this not-as-rare-as-you'd-think occurrence? Either swerve the car all over the road or speed up, then slam on the brakes. Our hood surfer experiences both forces here: swerving left to right and back again creates a centrifugal force, which can throw the crook off the side of the hood. Also, by speeding up and then abruptly stopping, inertia casts the offender forward, off the hood.

Now imagine the thrown man as blood and the car as a bloody hand, baseball bat, or other object, and you have a clear analogy of the creation of cast-off bloodstain patterns.

Let's bring these concepts back to a bloody crime. When a bludgeon weapon is used to beat a victim, that weapon has to be swung in an arc to do the damage. As it's swung back and again when brought forward, centrifugal force is at work pulling the blood off of it along the route. These drops create a line corresponding with the arc's path.

At the end of the back swing, the weapon stops suddenly before starting the forward swing to hit the victim. Inertia is at play at this point, the sudden stop pulling more blood droplets off. Every new swing in the beating creates a new line of centrifugal cast-offs and inertial blood patterns.

Centrifugal cast-off patterns might be caused by:

- The overhead backswing of a bat/axe/club.
- The forward swing of the bat/axe/club.
- The side-to-side slashing of a knife.
- Throwing a bloody hand up to defend against a blow.

Inertial cast-offs might be caused by:

- The sudden stop between the back and forward swings of a bludgeon.
- Any defensive movement that stops a blade mid-swing.
- A forward thrust of the weapon.

> PITFALL – Clean weapons don't create cast-offs. Until there is an injury that coats the weapon with blood, it cannot create bloodstain patterns. The initial swing/swipe/strike is clean. Only subsequent blows will create cast-offs in your scene.

Other Patterns

There are two other types of Spatter Patterns to discuss, both of which are created by the body itself. The first is created by its own internal force, which we call blood pressure. It's that force, created by the heart, which moves our blood throughout the body and also makes us bleed when a vein, artery or capillary is breached. The pressure is greatest in the arteries, which carry the blood away from the heart to the rest of the body. If an artery is severed, the blood is forcibly ejected, often as a spray, from the body. This spray, called **Arterial spurts**, can make its own unique bloodstain pattern as it often forms arches on the wall. The arches correspond with the heartbeat.

Figure 13: Arterial spurt pattern

The other body-created Spatter Stains, called **Expirated bloodstain patterns**, can be misleading as they often show a "misting" very similar to that of a high velocity impact spatter pattern. Expirated blood is blood that has pooled in a victim's lungs or airway. As the victim struggles for breath, the air in the lungs mixes with the blood and it is breathed out as a cloud. So, expirated bloodstain patterns are from actual blood mist that's created by the body, while the high velocity impact spatter creates droplets so small they mimic misting.

Figure 14: Expirated bloodstain

Although these two stains can look very similar, evaluation of the victim and the scene should readily point the investigator in the right direction. The high velocity impact spatter scene should also contain other evidence of firearms, such as the entrance/exit wounds on the victim as well as the hole the bullet caused in the wall or other item on its trajectory. Expirated blood stays right around the victim's nose and mouth, so any stain should be right near the victim's face.

Altered Stains

Altered Stains are just that – "altered." They are not produced by the injury itself or cast off during the incident. Instead, these stains are to some degree changes of the original bloodstain pattern. Whether the blood was transferred to a wall because a bloody hand brushed against it or there was some attempt at cleaning up, the final bloodstains are not the original bloodstains. There are several types of Altered Stains.

A **contact pattern**, or **pattern transfer**, is a type of transfer stain pattern in which a bloody object leaves an impression on a non-bloody surface. Bloody hand prints are an example of a contact pattern.

Figure 15: Bloody hand print contact pattern

Many contact patterns leave the shape of their

CHAPTER 3: TYPES OF PATTERNS

parent object as the stain, and can therefore identify the type of object that created it. For example, if a hammer was used as the weapon and became covered in blood, and then was set down on the kitchen counter, away from where the beating happened, the blood left on the counter would be in the shape of a hammer's head. Belt buckles, shoe patterns and paw prints are other examples of contact patterns.

Figure 16: Bloody shoeprint contact pattern

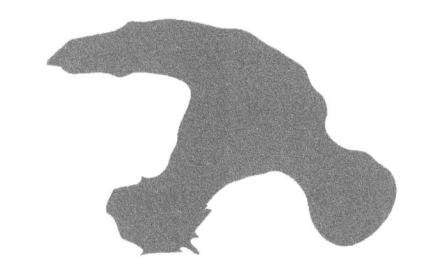

Figure 17: Bloody hammer contact pattern

A **Swipe** is a transfer pattern that occurs when a bloody surface rubs across a clean surface. The difference here is with a contact pattern the bloody object leaves its impression behind, while in a swipe, just a stroke of blood is left.

Figure 18: Swipe pattern

The direction of motion can be determined in swipes. Typically, more blood is left at the initial contact side of the pattern than on the side where the object lost contact with the surface. This is because as more blood is deposited as the swipe progresses, there is less blood for the rest of the swipe.

Think of when you put a paintbrush into some paint. When you put the paint on the wall, the first stroke will leave the greatest amount of paint at the initial contact point. If only one stroke is made, the brush runs out of paint at the end of the stroke. That's why we brush back and forth over the area before going back to the can for more paint, to spread all of the paint evenly.

In the case of a swipe, there is only the one stroke, with the paint barely present at the end of it. That uneven end section is said to have a "feathering" effect, where the paint (or in our case, blood) tapers away. In this way, feathered margins are a good indication of motion. The bloody object swiped the wall towards the feathered edge of the stain.

Figure 19: Feathering effect as the blood runs out, showing which direction the swipe was made

Another type of transfer pattern, a **Wipe**, differs from a swipe in that it occurs when a non-bloody surface moves through a bloody one. In a swipe, the blood in the stain was introduced by the object. In a wipe, the object is traveling through blood already present on the surface. So, while a swipe looks simply like a stroke of blood, a wipe also includes the source of the blood, the original pool, as part of the stain, with the stroke emerging from it.

Figure 20: Wipe Pattern

Keep in mind the "pool" could be as small as a

droplet. So, if a swipe is like putting paint on a wall from a brush, a wipe would be like dragging a dry mop through a puddle of water on the floor. The mop did not add the water to the floor, and the puddle is part of the final wipe pattern. As with swipes, wipes have a feathering effect that occurs as the blood is used up, and the feathering points in the direction of the movement. Wipes not only occur when the victim or suspect inadvertently traverses through deposited blood, but also when the suspect attempts to clean up.

> **TERMS – Tricky terminology – Swipes vs Wipes.** Both of these Altered Stains are similar, but differ in their creation. A swipe is created when a bloody object brushes onto a non-bloody surface. Think of paint brushed on a wall. A wipe is from blood already existing on the surface that is spread by the smearing of it by a non-bloody object. Think of a dry mop pulled through a pool of liquid on the floor. A swipe and a wipe have similar patterns, but different origins.

Each droplet dries from the outer edge inward, with the center being last to dry. The edges of each individual droplet bloodstain will start to dry within the first few minutes of landing on the surface. If someone attempts to wipe up the scene after the drying process has started, what happens is the center part (which is still liquid) is wiped away, but the outer dried ring is left, leaving a donut-shaped stain. These blood rings require a bit more effort to clean up and are often overlooked. Finding blood rings at a scene almost always indicates that a cleaning attempt was made. This can dispel most theories that the victim committed suicide, as the deceased are terrible at housekeeping.

Figure 21: Ring pattern of dried blood left when the liquid blood in the center was wiped away

> **PROCEDURE – A dried ring of blood with an empty center almost always means someone tried to clean up.**

Animal activity is important to note in scenes with Altered Stains. In these cases, the Altered Stains may not have anything to do with the crime itself, but exist simply because a pet was active in the scene. Certain swipes that seem significant may simply be where a house cat brushed fur matted with blood against the wall. A wipe might have occurred when the dog laid down in the bloody scene. There is also insect activity present at most scenes. Flies can transfer blood around the scene, creating several minute spatter patterns that an untrained investigator can incorrectly assess as important.

> ACCURACY – Pets can significantly alter the stains CSIs need to make an accurate analysis. Fluffy can be a dog-gone pain if running amok in a bloody scene. Confusing patterns can be caused by the cutest of culprits.

Passive Stains

There are many types of **Passive Bloodstains** that occur because of gravity or other environment factors, independent of the blood-inducing incident.

Drip patterns are a result of gravity and occur when blood drips into blood. As we discussed in the last chapter, a drip caused by gravity will fall perpendicular to the ground (straight down) and hit the surface at a 90-degree angle. This causes a circular stain. The next drip that falls into the circular stain of the first drip creates the drip pattern. The result of a liquid striking a liquid is several spines radiating out from the main drop as well as many tiny satellites thrown around the main drop. Therefore, drip patterns are also called satellite staining.

We previously touched on another situation in

which satellite staining occurs, but without a drip-into-drip impact. The type of surface a liquid strikes has a monumental effect on the stain it produces. The liquid will always want to form a circular stain (because of its surface tension), and that is what you'll get on hard, nonporous surfaces, like glass, bathroom tile or marble counter tops. However, rough or irregular surfaces, such as unsanded wood, concrete or leather, will create a much more unstable stain whose shape can vary wildly. These surfaces can also create satellite staining without the aid of an additional drip striking it.

Figure 22: Normal passive drip pattern when landing on a hard, nonporous surface

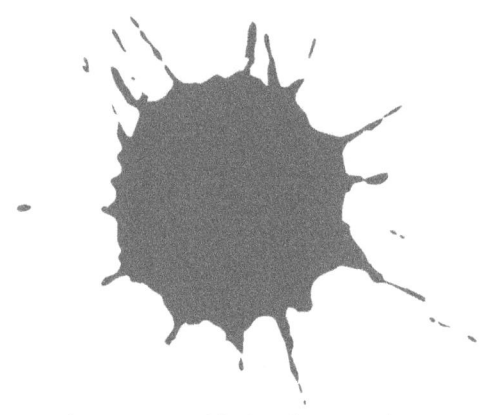

Figure 23: Complexities are added to the stain if it lands on a rough, uneven or porous surface

A **flow pattern** bloodstain occurs when the original blood deposit has enough blood in it that gravity (or sometimes movement) can affect it by pulling it in a downward path. This is simply a liquid acting like a liquid, just as when gravity pulls water down a slope to create a stream. A pool of blood on a steep driveway will be pulled down to the lowest area it can flow into. Likewise, blood on a wall will be pulled towards the floor, away from the original impact site.

A flow pattern is a long, narrow "finger" traveling away from the originating stain. Often, stains can have several flow patterns emerging from them, although they all move downward. Gravity is constantly at work, so most of the blood is eventually pulled away from the parent pool, meaning the stain is the thickest at the ends of the fingers.

Chapter 3: Types of Patterns

Figure 24: Flow pattern fingers

There are two items of importance that investigators need to keep in mind when they come across a flow pattern. First, a flow pattern is a change of the scene. The natural force of gravity pulled the blood away from where it originally landed. Therefore, where the blood ended up (at the end of the fingers) should not be considered when attempting to reconstruct the crime. The location of the parent pool holds the analytical significance.

Second, in any scene where the flow goes against gravity, that scene has been tampered with. If a body is on its back and the blood seems to have flowed from the base of the skull up past the ear to the temple area, that body has been turned over after death, or more specifically, after the blood had already flowed down.

> PITFALL – Blood never flows up. Gravity only works in one direction.

Miscellaneous Stains

There is one type of "stain" that doesn't fit the above categories but is very important to an investigation. I say "stain" (in quotations) because it actually isn't a stain at all. It's the lack of stains. **Void patterns** are areas within a bloody scene that logic would dictate should have blood, but none is present. If there is a significant amount of blood on an area of a wall, but right in the middle of that blood the wall is completely clean, that is more than likely a void pattern.

Void patterns are created when an object is in the way and stopped that blood from reaching the surface with the rest of the stain. If a lamp was in front of the wall, it would have stopped some of the blood getting on the wall and would have caused a "shadow" of itself where the wall was clear of blood. If the lamp was still there at the time the scene was being processed by CSIs, the void pattern would be easily explained and the lamp would be of little significance. It's the situations where there are void patterns but the bloody objects are missing that the investigators need to try to identify what the objects were and why they're gone. Void patterns can often be used to estimate the size and shape of the objects that caused them.

Figure 25: A void pattern. A hammer was present when the blood pattern was created

> **ACCURACY** – Remember, sometimes where blood *isn't* is as significant as where it is.

So now we've covered how blood acts and the different patterns it forms. In the next chapter, we'll take all of this and view it through the perspective of actual crime scene investigators to see how they put the puzzle together in their scenes.

Chapter 4: Processing the Scene

In the last three chapters, we've gone over the particulars of blood spatter analysis. We've discussed the proper terminology, how a liquid reacts in different situations and the categories of bloodstains. That's the backdrop to the actual process. In this chapter, you'll see how it all comes together: what real life investigators do in bloody scenes and how they use the blood spatter to tell the tale, so you can write your fictional professionals realistically.

Bloodstain Pattern Analysts

Just who are these bloody heroes capable of taking pattern stains back through time to their inception? Most people associate Dexter Morgan, the lead character of the television series *Dexter*, with bloodstain pattern analysts. On that show, Dexter was a forensic technician who specialized in blood spatter analysis. That's completely plausible.

In reality, the field of bloodstain pattern analysis has been fairly unregulated. That's not to say the field was open to those without qualifications, just that historically, no regulation has required a specific, consistent qualification for any particular agency. While that is changing, it has pretty much been up to each law enforcement entity, be it police department, sheriff's office, state police force or federal agency, to determine who is qualified to conduct that examination for their cases. If an agency does not have a specialist or the budget to train their own, they call in an expert, either paid or borrowed to assist in their investigation. The problem with non-regulation, however, is it opens the door for sloppy work at the hands of those without proper training.

In the last ten years, many national organizations have instituted very strict training requirements for blood spatter analysts. The International Association for Identification lists the following qualifications:

- Forty hours of blood spatter analysis training from a certified school or provider.
- Forty hours of crime scene photography training from a certified school or provider.
- 160 hours of training in the following courses from a certified school or provider:
  - Crime scene investigation technology.
  - Evidence recovery.
  - Blood detection techniques.
  - Medicolegal death investigations.
  - Forensic science and technology.
- Three years of practice within the bloodstain pattern identification discipline.

- A six-hour examination covering the following sections:
  - Written examination testing:
    - Bloodstain pattern analysis terminology.
    - Bloodstains and bloodstain patterns recognition.
    - Wound pathology.
    - Investigative and scene reconstruction procedures.
    - Crime Scene processing.
    - History of bloodstain pattern analysis.
    - Bloodstain pattern analysis theory and logic.
    - Mathematics (Basic understanding pertaining to discipline applications).
  - Pattern identification.
  - Analysis portion.
  - Area of convergence and point of origin calculations.

As you can see, these strict requirements make this forensic field a specialized job, but more importantly regulate the analysts to ensure the testimonies given in court are both accurate and reliable.

Processing Bloodstains

Preparation

Let's remember that for any blood spatter analysis to occur there first must be, well, *blood*. Whether doctor, coroner or blood drive volunteer, whenever people work around blood, they must maintain awareness of potential hazards.

Bloodborne pathogens present a real risk to anyone who does not guard against them. So at a bloody crime scene, before any processing occurs, all people who have any authority to enter need to suit up in Personal Protective Equipment (PPE).

> TERMS – Bloodborne Pathogens are microorganisms within blood capable of causing diseases, such as Hepatitis C or the Human Immunodeficiency Virus (HIV).

PPE is any of a variety of outer layer disposable clothing. It consists of latex gloves, shoe booties, sleeves, goggles, aprons, masks and full bio-hazard "bunny" suits. Every piece of PPE is intended to create a barrier between potential pathogens and the person working around them.

Every law enforcement agency outfits their officers/agents with PPE. Responding officials often create a go-to bag, called a crime scene kit, which includes everything they need at most crime scenes. Crime scene kits can vary agency to agency but most often they include evidence collection materials (bags, jars, labels, markers), flashlights, pens, pads of paper, agency forms and PPE. The crime scene kit is often stored in the investigator's vehicle and is therefore always accessible when he/she responds to a scene. This way, whenever PPE is necessary, it is readily available to the investigator.

I am often asked how much PPE an investigator should put on. My standard answer is always, if you're concerned whether you are sufficiently protected, you *aren't*.

At a minimum gloves and booties should be worn at all times, but it does not make sense to me to fail to protect yourself adequately. While the vast majority of bloodborne pathogens die within a few minutes of being exposed to the environment outside the body, no one wants to encounter the first documented exception to that rule.

Crime scenes present many other complications and require additional preparations and procedures, but in this book, let's remain focused and only address the steps of identifying and assessing blood in the crime scene to conduct the blood spatter analysis.

> FUN FACT – Many heroes in books and shows walk into a scene as if they were walking into a social setting, hands bare and clothing exposed. Real life CSIs know PPE can protect the scene, the evidence, and perhaps their lives.

Considering The Big Picture

The first thing any good investigator does when entering a crime scene is to make a birds-eye assessment. What does the scene, as a whole, say happened? Focusing on only one area cannot give a full picture. It is just as unrealistic as overhearing one sentence of a discussion and believing you know what the conversation is about. Likewise, any investigator who rushes right up to a body in the middle of the floor is far too tunnel-visioned to process a scene. The body is the end result. The scene is the story of how it got there.

The same rule applies to blood spatter analysis. Going straight to an individual stain to start the analysis can lead the investigator to a premature assumption that can skew the overall assessment of the scene. Remember, one small bloodstain cannot produce a comprehensive blood spatter analysis. It is the overall picture, all of the stains working as one pattern, that pieces together and recreates the crime.

> ACCURACY – Blood spatter itself can only imply how many injuries occurred, not how many victims were involved. Multiple victims can only be determined through blood via DNA analysis or if the amount of blood exceeds what one person can provide.

This overall viewpoint should enable the trained investigator to form ideas of what happened – where the main violence took place, how the participants moved around after the fact and, particularly, if anything seems amiss or out of place, which would indicate either clean up or staging.

Documentation

In that vein, as with all other crime scenes, the next thing an investigator will do is take pictures of the blood spatter. This way the scene is preserved and each stain can be reevaluated later by other experts who may not be present, even if the scene has been released and cleaned.

Normally, each crime scene has a law enforcement officer who is assigned the duty of taking photographs, but there are times, mostly because of personnel issues, that they're taken by the lead investigator. Although an experienced crime scene photographer can take many of the standard pictures without supervision, all photographs are ultimately directed by the lead investigator.

Crime scene photography is its own topic because scene photos become such an essential part of the investigation. The problem with a photo, though, is unless it is married up with a very detailed photo log, specifics become questionable after time has passed. Sometimes years pass before photos are presented at a trial, and the clarity of the photographs' details can mean the difference between them aiding the case or being thrown out. Consider the confusion below with three scene photos:

- Why was this chair photographed?
- I see this is an up-close shot of a single blood droplet stain, but where in the room was it?
- Why is there a photograph of a blank wall?

Photographs should be able to tell the story of the scene on their own, so later on we know that the chair had some bloodstains on its lower leg, the close-up of the droplet was above the headboard in the master bedroom and the blank wall was showing a void pattern. To achieve this, a crime scene photographer follows a strict methodology for every desired shot.

Everything that the lead investigator wants photographed is done in three stages. First an **overall shot** is taken to show the room/area as a whole. Next, a **mid-range shot** establishes where in the overall scene this set of photos is focusing on. Finally **close-up shots** are snapped that show what the investigator wants captured. Several close-up shots are taken to make sure at least one is focused enough to analyze. Close-up shots also often include multiple shots with and without a ruler to convey scale.

So if the questioned photographs above were done correctly, the scene photographer would have taken the following sequences:

- An overall shot of the dining room, capturing as much of it as possible.

- A mid-range shot showing the chair in question (which is the photo mentioned above).
  - Several close-up shots of the spatter pattern on the lower leg with and without a ruler.
- An overall shot of the master bedroom, capturing as much of it as possible.
  - A mid-range shot showing the head of the bed, the headboard and the wall above it.
    - Several close-up shots of the blood droplet stain with and without ruler (one of which is the photo referred to above).
- An overall shot of the living room.
  - A mid-range shot of the far wall with spatter.
    - Several close-up shots of the blank area on the wall to show the void pattern (one of which is the above photograph).
    - This should lead investigators on a hunt for whatever object created the void pattern.

As stated above, after the photographs are under way, the investigator needs to take a breath, and *see*:

- What is the big picture?
- What is the scene trying to say?

- If they are in a house, does the blood seem limited to one room, or does it travel to other rooms?
- Is the blood generally around the body or significantly away from it?
- Do the observable injuries correspond with the general spatter patterns present?

All of these general pieces start to build the investigative puzzle.

Pattern Assessment

If the investigator is trained in bloodstain pattern analysis, or once the expert Blood Spatter Analyst arrives, individual patterns are evaluated. The trained eye learns a lot from bloodstain patterns simply by how they look. We discussed what the different patterns look like in the last chapter. Now, we're putting those patterns in a scene to see how the investigator evaluates them.

The investigator's goal is to reconstruct the crime. What does the blood say happened? What couldn't have happened to produce the patterns present? The reconstruction of the crime is invaluable so the investigators are not forced to solely rely upon a witness' or suspect's account, which are often untrue.

The easiest thing to determine about a pattern is what *level* of impact spatter occurred. Remember from last chapter – low velocity impact spatters are drips and flow patterns primarily caused by gravity, medium velocity impact spatters have individual stains smaller than a drip, and high velocity impact patterns have so many microscopic stains that the overall pattern looks like a mist.

> PROCEDURE – Low, Medium and High Velocity Impact Spatter categories are all easily distinguishable by the naked eye. Each category has unique injuries that cause the patterns.

The drips from low velocity impact spatter patterns are passive and create circular stains. These are important because these are droplets that came directly from the blood source, and were not flung off by another force.

When an investigator comes across passive drips without a blood source above them, the object the blood came from was moved. If this blood is from a person, it is most likely from the bleeding of an active wound. It could have come from the victim, if he/she was able to move around after the injury, but most times it is from the assailant. Investigators can track those drips and document movement throughout the scene.

These low velocity impact spatter patterns can be extremely valuable, not only to track movement in and around the scene for crime reconstruction, but also because if the stains are the suspect's blood, there is a chance to develop a DNA profile. Also, if they are the victim's blood dripping off the attacker, investigators may find that blood on the suspect's clothing if it wasn't properly cleaned or disposed of afterward.

In one of my cases, we found a young woman murdered in her bedroom. Most of the blood was in and around the bed, where her body was found. However, I also noticed a fair amount of passive bloodstains at the dresser, on the other side of the room. Because all of the blood found near the dresser was low velocity impact spatter, we knew that no struggle happened there. Remember, a struggle would have involved force greater than that of gravity, and the resulting stains would have been in the medium velocity impact category, and not passive drips.

The state of the scene also made it very unlikely that the victim was assaulted in her bed, got up and went to the dresser, and left all of the passive drips as she stood there, before getting back in bed to die. This meant the blood came from the assailant, and indicated something important to him was at that dresser. We know this because the number of circular stains at the dresser meant he spent time there, probably searching for whatever it was he needed. An investigator always needs to let the scene (in this case the blood) tell the story.

Knowing the blood couldn't have come from the

victim, and determining the attacker's actions based on the stains, gave the investigators the direction to focus their case. The investigation ultimately determined the murderer was someone the victim had just met and taken home with her. He was at the dresser after the murder looking for the piece of paper that he had written his telephone number on so he could eliminate any evidence that he had ever met the victim.

If there is enough blood at a scene to produce passive drips, there are likely (but not always) other blood patterns, created when the injury was inflicted. Medium velocity impact spatter patterns are normally produced at the time of injury, and become instrumental in the determination of where the injury occurred within the room, which we'll go over below in the next section. This is a major step in the crime reconstruction.

A trained investigator should be able to identify whether cast-off patterns exist. Cast-offs are the result of a medium velocity force and can be indicative of a beating or slashing.

> PROCEDURE – Spatter Stain cast-off patterns are lines of medium velocity impact spatter blood drops formed by swinging a bloody object. The number of lines correspond to the number of strikes, adding one for the initial blow.

Beatings are the easier of the medium velocity

impact spatter patterns to identify. There is typically enough blood present on the weapon to create full patterns. Last chapter, I explained the forces involved that create these cast-off patterns. Here, I want to talk about what the investigator sees and how those patterns are discovered.

A cast-off pattern is essentially a line of blood flung onto a surface. It is not a solid line. Instead, the line is made up of several droplets distributed along the same path. So the investigator more or less just "connects the dots" to see the course of the pattern and the vector of the force producing it.

Think about dipping a paintbrush into the paint and then sharply flicking your wrist once from right to left in front of a canvas. The result is a perfect cast-off pattern. Many paint drops were flung off of the brush, forming a line across the canvas. Now simply replace the canvas with a wall, ceiling or floor, replace the paint with blood, and replace the paintbrush with a bat, axe, hand or any other bloody object, and we're back in our crime scene.

CHAPTER 4: PROCESSING THE SCENE

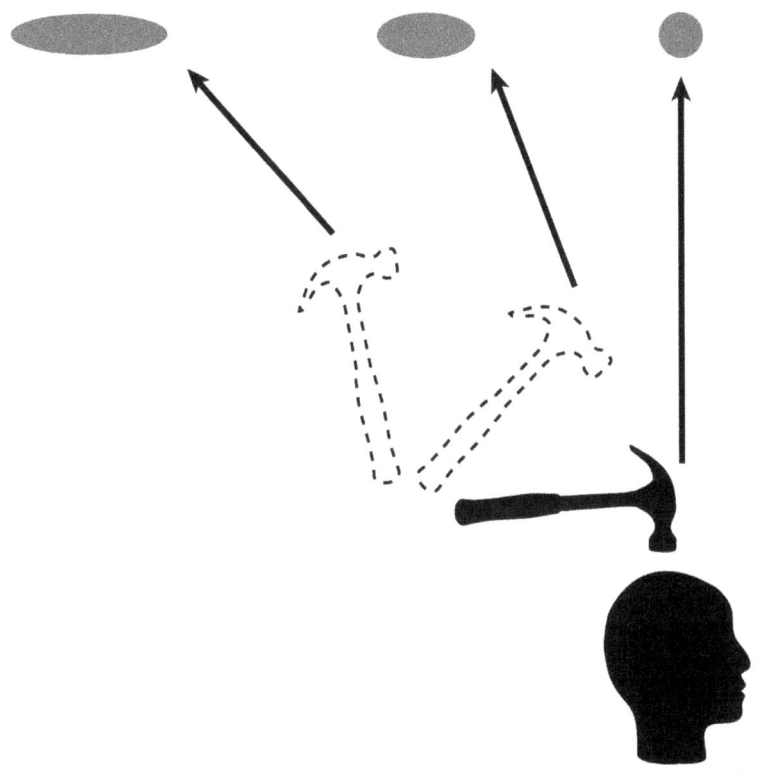

Figure 26: How a cast-off pattern is created – the smaller the angle of impact, the longer the stain

Every blow by the bludgeon creates a new cast-off line. In this way, an investigator can determine how many hits the suspect delivered to the victim. It's important to note, however, the first blow is what causes the injury, that is, what causes the victim to bleed. So, for that initial hit, the weapon is *free of blood*, and no cast-off pattern is created.

Every time the victim is hit after the first time, the instrument is re-covered in blood, making a very clear cast-off pattern for each swing. The investigator

77

simply counts the number of distinct cast-off line patterns at the scene and then adds one more to account for the first strike. That provides a very solid estimate of how many times the victim was hit.

Figure 27: Multiple cast-off patterns give a strong estimation of how many times the victim was hit

Slicing produces cast-off patterns that are a little bit different from the type seen after a beating, although the physics behind them are identical. When cutting someone, the assailant typically swings in a side-to-side motion, which has considerably less power than the over-the-head wind up found in a beating swing. Furthermore, a knife cuts because it is sharp, which offers considerably less surface area on which blood can collect.

These two factors typically mean that a slicing motion, while still creating cast-off patterns, has fewer blood drops within the overall line pattern than are seen in beating cast-offs. The line is still identifiable, but not as overtly obvious. Also, a slicing line tends to be horizontal due to the left/right swings, while a beating cast-off pattern tends to be overhead or diagonal on a wall.

None of these are hard-and-fast rules, and any scene could provide an exception, but generally this is what the investigator expects to find with medium velocity impact spatters.

If a misting pattern exists in the scene, the investigator knows its creation was from one of only two sources: either there was a force so great that the blood droplets were small enough for the resulting stain to resemble a mist, which is a high velocity impact spatter, or the stain was from a victim breathing out an actual bloody-air mist, creating an expirated bloodstain. When I say a misting pattern, that simply means the droplets are too small to identify individually and, from a distance, the result looks like the wall is stained pink.

> PROCEDURE – Misting patterns are either caused by high velocity impact spatter patterns, which require a force so explosive that the blood drops are infinitely small, or by an actual mist created by blood in the airway.

The investigator can very easily differentiate between a high velocity impact spatter and an expirated blood pattern. Remember, expirated blood patterns are created when a victim is still breathing and blood pools in his or her lungs or airway. The blood literally becomes a mist as it mixes with the air exhaled by the victim. As with all other mists, the expired blood will only travel as far as the breath carrying it, which is typically right at the face. So if there is a mist pattern that is not near a body, and especially if there is no blood in and around the nose and mouth of that body, that body did not create that misting pattern.

The force needed for a high velocity impact spatter is so great that it creates a **blowback**, which last chapter we also called back spatter. Unlike a medium velocity force, such as a stabbing or beating, which is localized on the body at the sight of the blow, in high velocity force situations there are two injuries: the site of the blow, called the **entrance wound**, and where the projectile leaves the body, called the **exit wound**. Blowback occurs at the entrance wound and, as the name indicates, is blood spatter expelled back, in the direction the force came from. The misting pattern in this situation is the blood thrown forward from the exit wound.

> ACCURACY – Back spatter, depending on the circumstances, will only travel four feet or less. A sniper will not be concerned about the victim's blood.

Finding both the blowback and forward stains can help give the investigator a rough estimate of where the person was when shot. If the person was shot at pointblank range, blowback very likely went onto the assailant him/herself. Blowback could be on the weapon, the assailant's hand, and also on his/her clothing, which he/she might not have checked thoroughly enough. Finding the victim's blood on a suspect is obviously vital evidence connecting the shooter to the scene.

Last chapter we also covered several stains that are unique and therefore easily identifiable for the investigator:

- **Arterial spurts** create arcing stains and mean an artery was cut.
- **Contact patterns** are stains in the shape of the bloody object that left them, such as belt buckles, hands, shoes, etc.
- **Swipes** and **Wipes** indicate movement through a scene.
- **Dried rings** suggest an attempt at cleaning up was made.
- **Void patterns** are areas free from stains where staining should have occurred. They often are in the shape of the object that intercepted the blood.

Many questions about what happened in a scene can be answered simply by the bloodstain patterns that are present:

- Are there flow patterns in the wrong direction, indicating the scene has been changed?

- Does there appear to be too much or too little blood based on the type of spatter or assumed injury?
- Is there any indication that a clean-up attempt has been made?

The patterns themselves help to focus the investigation and piece together what happened.

Crime Reconstruction

Once the general picture starts to take shape based on the overall scene examination, a true blood spatter analysis takes place. This is accomplished by someone specifically trained in that capacity and may require a specialist to be called to the scene. The specialist has blood spatter specific tools included in the crime scene kit. These would include adhesive rulers that can be placed on the floor or stuck on a vertical surface, a ball of string, a protractor and either a scientific calculator or a chart of mathematic tables.

A full-on blood spatter analysis takes several individual blood droplet stains within an overall pattern and determines where in three-dimensional space within the room the injury had to have occurred to produce that pattern. It tells investigators where, exactly, the blood came from. This is extremely beneficial in reconstructing the crime. There is a big difference between knowing the victim was shot and proving the victim was shot while sitting down, which would go against any claim that the shooter was in fear for his life and acted in self-defense.

In order to determine the blood's point of origin in the room, the path it followed from injury to stain must be identified. We call this path the **directionality** of the bloodstain. We touched on directionality in Chapter 2.

Each individual droplet stain shows directionality. A perfect circle indicates the drop fell straight down, while any differing angles of travel, creating ever-elongating oval stains, shows movement through the room.

Investigators use two methods to determine directionality in a bloodstain. First is what we discussed previously – the spine of the bloodstain. This is that minuscule cast-off that was created at impact and thrown ahead of the stain, and points in the direction the blood was traveling. So if we identify a spine, we know the blood came from the opposite direction.

Second, in most bloodstains, if you look at the front and the back points of the oval, one will be fairly crisp and smooth, while the other point will display a more jagged edge. The *smooth point* is always the point where the droplet first contacted the surface. The *irregular edge* is the forward end of the stain. It is created because the force still wants to carry the blood along, although there just is no more blood to go. So the jaggedness is created by the pull still acting on the stain, and is where most of the blood within the stain ended up. It always points in the direction the blood was going. As with the spine, the blood originated from the opposite direction.

> PROCEDURE – Directionality – Like a spine, a jagged edge of a bloodstain points in the direction the blood drop was traveling, so the incident happened in the opposite direction.

Using this directionality, if you were to draw a line lengthwise through the stain from jagged edge back to the smooth edge and then kept the line going, that line represents the pathway the blood traveled to get to that spot. If you were to draw similar lines in several other stains within the same pattern, there would be an obvious point where all of those lines come close to intersecting. That is called the **Area of Convergence** and identifies the general location at which the injury occurred. But be aware, this is simply a two-dimensional generalization.

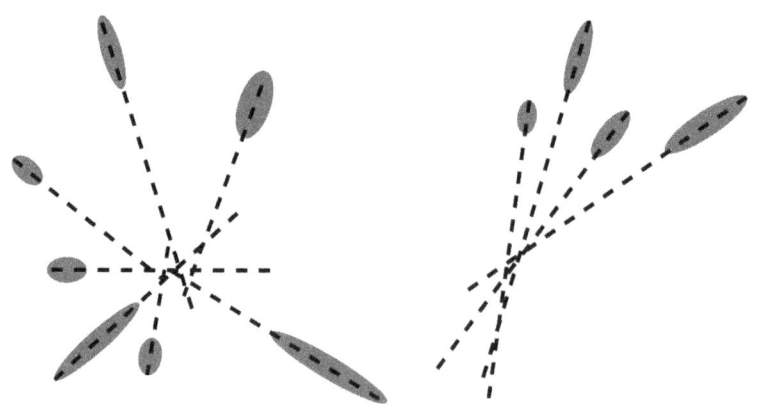

Figure 28: Area of convergence estimations for two types of patterns

If you were looking at a pattern on the floor, for example, those lines you drew would all be at the floor level, and the Area of Convergence also would be on the floor. But we know the injury did not happen at floor level. It happened somewhere above that area of the intersecting lines.

> PROCEDURE – Each stain's directionality gives you the Area of Convergence (Two-Dimensional). Each stain's directionality, along with the angle of impact, gives you the Point of Origin (Three-Dimensional).

So the real key in a bloodstain pattern analysis is to take the two-dimensional Area of Convergence and make it a three-dimensional **Point of Origin**. Unfortunately, this takes math. As an author, this might be too technical for your story and you may just want to tell your readers that your Bloodstain Specialist Superstar discovered the Point of Origin and gloss over the science and math of it all. But for those of you out there who need to research every nook and cranny of a subject (you know who you are!), here's the magic behind the curtain of blood spatter analysis.

> ALERT – The following section becomes more technical than most writers need for their stories. The mathematical equations ahead are provided for those who desire complete research data. Those needing just the essentials can skip ahead to the section on Outdoor Scenes.

Let's say we have a bloodstain pattern on a wall, about 4 – 5 feet above the floor. If we were to do a two-dimensional Area of Convergence determination, odds are it would be roughly in the center of those droplets. In order to take our analysis off of the wall and into the room, we have to determine the impact angle for *every* bloodstain we're evaluating.

Once the expert calculates the angle for a stain, a string is taped to the base of the stain and pulled out into the room at that angle. We know that blood drop traveled along this path in order to hit the wall at that determined angle. By figuring out and using the angle of impact, we have taken the line we drew for the Area of Convergence and lifted it off the wall at the proper angle so it can exist in space.

We follow this stringing technique for every impact angle we calculated for each individual bloodstain. All of the strings will intersect in the room and that is the Point of Origin, the place the injury had to have occurred within the room to produce that pattern on the wall.

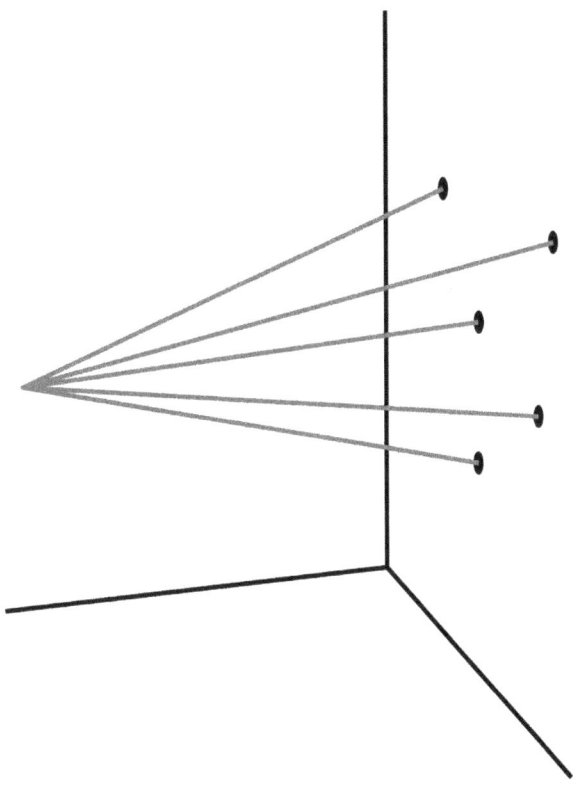

Figure 29: Point of origin determination

So, the most important step in determining the Point of Origin is calculating the **angle of impact**. This is possible because of the physics involved with liquids which we discussed in Chapter 2. Every drop of blood flung from a body will have surface tension working on it to make it spherical. This shape will always make an ellipse (oval) shape for the resulting stain for any angle other than a 90-degree free fall.

When there are constants in our lives, mathematical equations can be extrapolated to predict other occurrences of the same thing. In this case, the angle of impact can be determined by the length and width of the stain, which the investigator must measure. In many stains, as stated above, one edge can be rather irregular or jagged, making the point from which to measure the length unclear. To get the measurements, the CSI must eyeball a *perfect* oval within the stain. The jagged edge is not included in this calculation. Nor is any spine cast off in front of the stain or satellite staining around the bloodstain. All we worry about is the perfect oval of the stain itself. Keep in mind this becomes extraordinarily difficult as many stains can be incredibly tiny.

The math begins by dividing the width by the length. The arc sine is then taken of that answer to determine the degree of the angle of impact. I don't know of any crime scene investigator that can do an arc sine on the fly. Mostly we use a scientific calculator or have an arc sine table available to check. The arc sine answer is the angle of impact for that stain.

> **TERMS** – The arc sine is a mathematical function, taken from trigonometry, which calculates the angle of impact from a stain's width and length. For investigators, it's a button on the calculator.

A protractor is then used at the base of the bloodstain to make sure the string is at the correct angle. The entire process is repeated with the length and width measurements of every subsequent stain, until the number of stains you want evaluated are all stringed. Again, the location where all of the strings intersect is the Point of Origin that created that pattern.

One thing to consider when conducting a bloodstain pattern analysis is that there may only be one incident in that scene, creating one bloodstain pattern, but there also may be several incidents, creating multiple patterns that may even overlap. So, if one of the strings you're using to determine a Point of Origin goes off on its own, your investigator character needn't panic.

Always check your work as this is an exact specialty, but if it all checks out, you most likely found a drop from a different pattern that covers the same area. That just means that there was another injury inflicted that caused another pattern, all of which assists you in determining what happened during the crime.

Outdoor Scenes

I'm sure you've noticed that thus far, all of my discussions have involved indoor surfaces that include floors, walls and ceilings, with a lamp or two thrown in for good measure. But not all crimes happen inside. What happens when we take the blood-inducing event out the front door?

Mechanically, the physics are the same no matter

what environment exists around the events. So, a gunshot wound will produce the same high velocity impact spatter and back spatter as we discussed previously. There will still be cast-off spatter thrown from beatings. Active bleeding will still produce low velocity impact drips.

The difference, and the difficulty, when dealing with outdoor scenes is they are not self-contained, controlled environments with uniform surfaces. Think about any room in your home. If your loving spouse threw a glass of red fruit punch from a glass and made no attempt to clean or hide it, you'd see it immediately, whether it was on a hardwood floor or carpet, over a couch or on a wall. Using what you've learned in this book, you could begin analyzing the patterns immediately after you skinned your significant other alive.

Now, with that same glass of punch, have your loving mate throw it into the backyard. How easily can you find the stains this time if you were not around to see where they landed?

Nature is made up of multiple colors and textures, unlike the consistent look of our interior designs. The red liquid does not immediately reveal itself. Not to mention that a portion of the stain goes below the foliage/grass or is absorbed into the soil. Identifying a stain even exists can be incredibly difficult outside.

Also, outdoor environments have multiple surface

angles to distort the stain formation. Using the same backyard as above, each blade of grass is unique and not oriented in the same position as its neighboring blades. Having multiple surfaces like this makes an analysis incredibly difficult, because you cannot accurately compare one surface to another. How do you know the grass blade wasn't twisted by the blood, by your analysis or by some other intervening alteration such as being stepped on? On an interior wall, the entire surface is uniform. Outside that is hard to come by. Add to that any debris on the ground such as leaves, rocks or litter, and the number of potential surfaces becomes impossible to analyze.

Outdoor scenes do have cases of usable surfaces. Paved streets, sidewalks or driveways, for example. On these a stain should be readily identifiable. However, if the driveway is pitched, or the street/sidewalk are on a hill, gravity will take over after the stain has formed. This is where you will see the blood flow in the finger patterns down to the lowest point possible.

> ACCURACY – Bloodstain pattern analysis works the same outdoors as it does indoors, if you can find a viable pattern. Surface variances, weather and additional activity within the scene make identifying and conducting a pristine analysis challenging.

Some outdoor surfaces work just as well as interior ones do. These can be the exterior walls of buildings, the tops of picnic tables or the sides of cars. They all work great for blood spatter analysis. But, open-air scenes come with other complications, including weather. Any sort of rain will wash some or all of the pattern away. We're dealing with liquids here. Strong winds can affect the trajectory of the droplets before they hit a surface. Scorching heat can dry the stain so entirely that it has flaked off before it can be recorded.

Yet another complication of having blood out of the controlled environment of a building is additional activity within the scene. Blood on a street can be driven over. Blood on a beach can be washed away. Blood in the open can have all sorts of animal activities. Blood attracts many form of insects from flies (which lay eggs in dead bodies, a source of non-ending nourishment to the larvae) to beetles (which eat fly larvae). Some larger animals, such as neighborhood dogs or wild coyotes, can also be attracted to blood. Any sort of animal activity within the scene alters it, and may do so to a significant degree.

> **PROCEDURE** – Tracking (mostly drips or swipes) is a reliable use of blood found outdoors.

One type of outdoor blood analysis used often in storytelling that does work well is tracking movement. Passive drips, even on pitched driveways, create a path investigators can follow. Swipes on foliage through an overgrown swamp or dense forest, or on walls or fences in more urban areas, can provide a trail that leads your characters to their next important find.

Now that you've learned what the real life professionals do with the types of blood spatter patterns in their scenes, next chapter we will adapt that to fit into your fictional worlds.

Exercise: Shower Spatter

One very easy exercise you can do at home to create your own spatter patterns will give you an opportunity to identify and conduct a quick pattern analysis for yourself. If you have a glass shower door, all you need to do is treat yourself to a nice hot shower. If you don't have a glass shower, an easy substitute is a steamy bathroom mirror.

Once you have a good steam going so that the shower door or mirror fogs over entirely, just take your wet hand and flick your fingers open in the direction of the glass to create your very own spatter pattern, which will probably look a lot like this:

Figure 30: DIY Shower Spatter

As you already know, this is a medium velocity impact spatter, as the force created by your fingers was greater than gravity (therefore greater than a low velocity impact spatter), and there is no way for your body to create enough force to create a high velocity impact spatter.

You can take a lot of information from this homemade spatter, and the great news is you already *know* the correct answers since you were there at the pattern's creation!

The movement of each finger created a centrifugal

force that created a cast-off pattern in the form of lines moving away from the center of the pattern. You should be able to count four distinct lines, one for each finger. In a bloody scene, each line would indicate a different swing of the weapon.

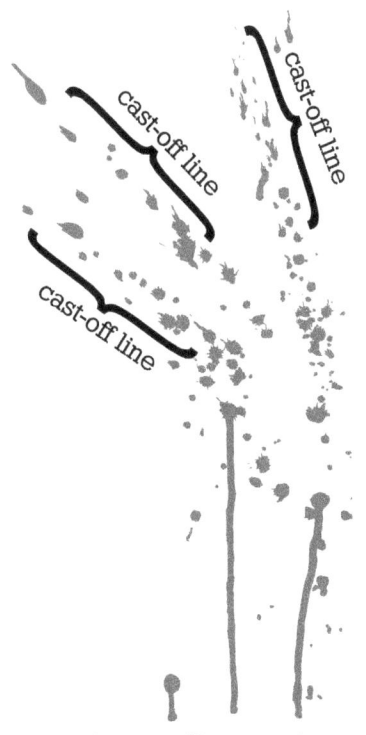

Figure 31: Recognizing the cast-off patterns in your shower spatter

Your fingers also used inertia when they suddenly stopped to cast off more drops right at the level of the flick.

In the midst of those cast-offs, where most of the water hit the glass, you should see gravity at work, causing flow pattern "fingers." This is the pattern left as the water begins to be pulled down to the floor. This is a passive stain and was not caused by the incident (in this case your finger flicking), but instead occurred after the fact by gravity.

On the outer edges of the pattern you should see individual droplets that are more elongated than the 90-degree patterns. You should be able to see and identify the spines that leapt out in front of the droplets, which points you in the direction that each droplet was traveling in.

Figure 32: Identifying the spines and flow fingers in your shower spatter

EXERCISE: SHOWER SPATTER

Now is your opportunity to become a Pattern Analysis expert! Take all of the outer-edge droplets you can identify and determine each of their directions. Then follow the opposite direction to the point where they all intersect. You've just found your first Area of Convergence! And to check your work, that point should be at the same level that your hand was when you did the flick! And that's what an Area of Convergence tells you: the spot on the two-dimensional surface that corresponds to where the incident happened.

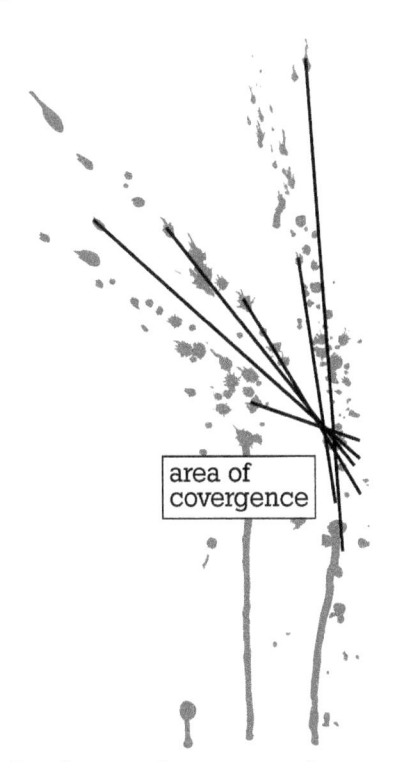

Figure 33: Finding the area of convergence in your shower spatter

Asking you to do a full-on Point of Origin mathematical exercise just seems cruel, but with everything you've identified above, I'd say you're well on your way to analyzing your own (fictional) scenes!

Case Study #2: Bret Harris – The Blood Doesn't Lie

Bret Harris was a troubled young man who had spent many years of his adolescence in and out of jail. He had documented mental-health issues and at one time had been committed to the Napa State Hospital, near Sacramento, CA. In 1982 he was released from the hospital into his mother's care. Two years later, twenty-four year old Bret called 911 reporting his mother and stepfather were dead.

Neighbors and friends all indicated that Barbara Harris Gisler, 55, and Bob Gisler, 52, were happy together and tried to help Bret when they could. Records show Bob bailed Bret out of jail on several occasions and hired him to work at his tool-making company. Bret, on the other hand, seemed discontented and generally detached from his family.

On October 18, 1984, at 1:30 AM, Bret called 911 and said his mother had been murdered. During the call, Bret said his stepfather was also dead and Bret threatened to take his own life. When the Sacramento County Sheriff's Department deputies arrived, they discovered Bret attempting to hide in a tree. They ordered him down and entered the residence.

In the master bedroom, they found Barbara and Bob dead in a very bloody scene. Barbara was in the bed and Bob was lying face-up on the floor. Both had been severely beaten on the upper body and head, to the point to which their faces were unrecognizable. Autopsies later showed their arms were broken. Blood covered the walls and ceiling, the cast-off patterns revealing the unrelenting severity of the attacks. A bloody box cutter was found on Bob's chest, and a wooden axe handle had been thrown with such force that it protruded from the wall. Bloody footprints were found leading from the bedroom to an open drawer in the kitchen.

In Bret's initial interview after being taken out of the tree, he told the deputies that earlier that night he heard Barbara and Bob arguing in their bedroom. He said he ignored the fight as best he could until he heard his mother scream. Bret claimed he ran to their bedroom and discovered Bob standing over his mother's body. Bret said he saw the axe handle on the floor and grabbed it before Bob attacked him with the box cutter.

Bret admitted to beating Bob to death, but claimed it was an act of self-defense. In an attempt to corroborate his story, Bret showed investigators cuts on his body, on the inside of his left arm, on his chest and on his right cheek. Each cut was superficial, meaning they were all just on the surface of the skin, not deep enough to cut a vein or artery, and caused no more than minimal injury.

In a full out fight involving a sharp weapon, cuts tend to be deep and significant. While scrapes and nicks are possible, every cut leaving merely a superficial wound cast great doubt on Bret's story. The crime scene itself, tore his tale apart.

Bret claimed he entered the room after Bob had already killed Barbara, but the blood in the room did not support that account. The beatings were done with such ferocity that blood was flung everywhere in that room, saturating the walls, ceiling and floor. When Bob's body was transported out of the room, however, investigators discovered the carpet underneath him was clean. This meant the body laid there, creating a void pattern by protecting that patch of carpet from the later blood that coated that area.

Inspection of Bob's clothing revealed Barbara's blood on the front of his pajamas, but not on the back, which was against the carpet. This meant that Barbara's blood was added after Bob's body was down, getting on Bob's front but not on his back or the area of the floor that his body shielded. If Barbara's blood came after Bob was down, that meant Bob was killed first and Bret's story was a lie. He was charged with two counts of first-degree murder.

When confronted with this evidence back at the Sheriff's Office, Bret decided to change his story. He began muttering about "the Devil." He admitted to killing both of his parents but claimed they had been possessed by warlocks and his actions were still in self-defense. Unsurprisingly, Bret later entered a plea of not guilty by reason of insanity, most likely in an attempt to avoid jail and other punishments.

In most insanity defense cases, the burden falls on the defendant (the one claiming insanity) to prove that he/she was insane. That means the assumption is the defendant is sane until he/she reaches a specified level of proof to be considered otherwise. Although Bret did have documented treatment for mental-health issues, his new version of the events felt even flimsier than his original story. If this was truly a self-defense case, why did Bret attempt to hide upon law enforcement's arrival? If he actually believed his parents were possessed, and therefore he was justified in the killings, why did he make up a previous story?

Investigators then set out to show Bret was rational in his thinking that night, meaning he was fully aware his actions during the incident were wrong. An insane person is incapable of realizing these actions are wrong when subject to the delusions. Autopsies showed the severity of the beatings. All of the blows were to the upper bodies, heads and arms. In a full-out struggle, injuries tend to be found over an entire body. This doesn't by itself prove the victims did not fight back, but it again casts some doubt on Bret's account.

Further, both arms on both victims were severely broken in multiple places. This is typically considered a defensive wound, as a person instinctively throws up his/her arms to block an object on course to impact him/her. Defensive wounds are not always expected when the person is the aggressor, as Bret claimed. Again, this is not enough to choreograph what actually happened or to prove that Barbara or Bob was never the aggressor that evening, but it does not seem to fit seamlessly with Bret's story. What the number of blood spatter cast-off patterns, the amount of blood in the room, the location of the injuries and the intensity of the injuries revealed was that this encounter was vicious and was about obliterating, not subduing.

Probably the most damning evidence against Bret was the superficial cuts on his body. He had one on his right cheek, one on his chest and several on the inside of his left arm. The arm cuts were the most troubling. As stated above, when a person is trying to ward off an attack, that person instinctively throws up his/her arm to block it. The arm is where injuries are expected. However, in a confrontation with a sharp object such as a box cutter, those injuries should exist on the *outside* of the arm. All of Bret's arm cuts were on the *inside* of his arm. No one, insane or not, runs up to an attacker with his palms and inner elbows facing the knife. Cuts on an inner arm are almost without exception *self-inflicted*. If a person wants to cut him/herself, the inner arm is much more convenient than the outer side. Add to that the cuts were all superficial, and there were no cuts on the right arm at all, and it made sense that all of these injuries were caused by Bret himself while holding the box cutter in his right hand.

Once the wounds were determined to be self-inflicted, law enforcement could show that Bret actively and purposely tried to change the scene in an attempt to deceive police. Those are actions of a rational person, not someone in the throes of an insanity induced episode.

Had Bret believed his mom and stepfather were warlocks, he would not have had to cover it up. Prosecutors believed he entered Bob and Barbara's room with the intent to kill them. He attacked Bob first, who ended up on the bedroom floor. He then subdued his mother in the bed. Then he beat them both savagely.

After he was done, he threw the axe handle into the wall and walked to the kitchen, leaving bloody footprints behind him. He found a box cutter in the utility drawer, barely cut himself in an attempt to claim self-defense and then left the box cutter on top of Bob's chest, an improbable resting place for an item after a struggle. Eventually he called 911.

When presented with all of the evidence, Bret Harris withdrew his insanity plea and pleaded guilty to one count of first-degree murder and one count of second-degree murder, resulting in a sentence of forty-one years to life.

Blood spatter analysis was essential for the quick disproving of Bret's initial story. By listening to the story the blood told, investigators did not have to rely on Bret's ill-conceived lies. The blood led to the rightful conviction of a guilty man.

Chapter 5: Writing Your Scene

The secret to a well-crafted story is for a writer to solve the crime on paper before committing it *to* paper. You need to know how your characters are going to resolve the crime before you write the commission of it.

Far too often, one can get caught up in the sensationalism of the scene itself when writing a story chronologically from beginning to end. When it's time to write the endgame, though, writers may find themselves stuck, unprepared to "solve" their case and confused about what evidence will suddenly appear that resolves the investigation dramatically and clearly.

Identifying the solution *before* writing the crime allows the author to commit the crime mindfully and then leads the main characters to a convincing conclusion. Sloppy planning leads to in-story logic leaps and unsatisfying finales.

> PITFALL – Don't use bloody logic leaps! Having two gallons of blood present at the scene should not lead your protagonist to the conclusion that he has a serial killer who drains her victims dry. A much more logical assumption would be that she attacked more than one victim.

Likewise, I urge everyone reading this blood spatter book not to make the scene bloody for bloody's sake. Take the time to plot out what happened before writing the crime scene so the appropriate spatter patterns are present.

One baseball bat strike will not spray blood all over the room, just as a bloody hand print won't be left by an assailant who shot the victim from several feet away. In this chapter, we'll tackle different categories of bloodstains, their contributions to a fictional crime scene and consider scenarios in your story that might cause them. At the end, I will also provide a detailed menu for producing bloody crime scenes along with a streamlined chart that illustrates what weapons and actions create which bloodstains. We'll make your red stuff earn its paycheck.

> PITFALL – Make sure your scene matches your action. The walls won't be blood soaked from a paper cut.

You may feel as if there are an awful lot of rules when it comes to blood:

- How does it act?

- What shape does it form?
- What force needs to be present?
- What has been altered?

Don't be overwhelmed. Always remember that your story takes place in *your* world and you decide which rules work for you and which don't. You have the final say. Using blood in your story doesn't have to be an all-out or go-home affair.

Start with practicalities: what is your genre and what works for your story?

Maybe you're a horror writer who needs a gory scene painted so red that blood is dripping from the ceiling. Or perhaps you're brewing up a murder mystery or thriller, with only enough blood to identify a suspect. Or maybe your book's a paranormal, where the monster groupie lured an aloof vampire or shifter to her bungalow by slicing her hand. Blood works in all of these stories, but it leaves very different types of bloodstain patterns in each.

> **PITFALL** – Make sure the appropriate injuries are on your victim to match the bloodstain patterns. If there is a high velocity impact spatter, remember the victim should have been shot. If there is an Arterial Spurt pattern, remember the victim needs to have a severed artery.

Your first step when writing the bloody scene is to decide what deed put the blood there. In the dripping ceiling example above, you'll need an action that throws blood everywhere in great amounts, so I'm thinking a chainsaw, or perhaps a wood chipper. In the murder mystery, maybe your victim was stabbed to death, so a few horizontal cast-off patterns would work with a pool of blood near the body. For the sliced hand, the paranormal investigator would discover several passive drips on the floor, and maybe a swipe on the doorknob.

> PITFALL – Remember time marches on! If you're going to have blood drip onto your detective as he enters the scene, he probably should be arriving shortly after the incident occurred, or the blood would have already dripped. Gravity doesn't take a break.

Spatter Menu

Once you decide what the injury-inducing action is, your scene will almost paint itself. To aid you in that endeavor, I'm going to present you with a list of questions, which, when answered, will provide a menu of actions to choose from in order to produce the correct blood patterns in your scene. If you answer "yes" to any one, read the descriptions that follow to determine what blood spatter patterns should be present in your scene. If you answer "no" to a question, skip to the next one. There can be as many "yes" answers or "no" responses as your scene requires. Each time you write a new scene, the answers may change completely.

Is There A Gunshot Wound?

The force behind a gunshot wound makes it different from any other wound for two reasons: it creates two injury sites, and it produces a high velocity impact spatter pattern.

Almost every other type of injury happens at the site of impact, but for a bullet, the force is so great that the projectile is carried through the body, creating the entrance wound and the exit wound. There are instances where there is no exit wound and the bullet remains inside the body. If you want this to occur to your shooting victim, I recommend researching the circumstances needed for it. In most shooting cases, the bullet leaves the body.

All shooting victims will have an entrance wound, which is also called a **grazing wound** if the bullet doesn't enter. At this injury site the force of the bullet sprays blood backward a few feet, in the direction it came from, creating back spatter.

Back spatter is a medium velocity impact spatter pattern that produces a random array of blood droplets. Where back spatter becomes significant in investigations is in situations where the shooter is at very close to pointblank range. Back spatter will only travel three to four feet, maximum.

If close enough, the back spatter can cover the weapon, the shooter's hand, and perhaps up the arm. It can spatter his clothing or may only land on his shoes. Wherever it's found, back spatter provides an invaluable evidence link between the shooter and victim, proving the shooter was in very close proximity to the victim at the time of the shooting. Back spatter on a suicide shooter's hand has also been used to position the hand as a result of a Point of Origin determination in order to prove the shot was self-administered.

As discussed, the forward force of a bullet is immense and carries the bullet through the body. When the bullet creates the exit wound, the amount of force present makes the blood droplets microscopically tiny. This is why the resulting high velocity impact spatter resembles mist. The wall should appear stained pink and there should also be a hole in the wall where the bullet entered.

Is There A Beating (By Hand)?

A beating by hand does not normally produce any blood spatter patterns because it doesn't break the skin. Most injuries in this type of beating are internal. The two notable exceptions are the nose and mouth.

The teeth act as a solid barrier for the force of the punch to collide with. The lip is smashed in between, often times tearing. The initial hit to the mouth can throw blood a considerable distance if the face turns with the blow. If the blood hits a wall or other object, it creates a random pattern of medium velocity impact spatter.

Once the wound is bleeding, it can cause drip patterns around the scene, although many times the blood is taken into the mouth instead of falling to the ground. If enough blood is taken into the mouth and the victim is able to spit it out, that will also create a medium velocity impact spatter pattern.

A nosebleed can produce more bleeding than a mouth wound. As with being hit in the mouth, the initial nose strike will throw a medium velocity random pattern out. This injury also almost always creates drip patterns on the ground, as the blood is significant and slow to stop. Unless the nose bleed is stopped up by a tissue or rag, it will drip to the floor with regularity. If the person with the nosebleed moves around the scene, investigators can later follow those movements by tracking the drip patterns.

> FUN FACT – Nosebleeds bleed so much because the front of the nose is vascularized by an abundance of arteries and veins. This area, called Kiesselbach's plexus, is located on either side of the septum.

Is There A Beating (By Instrument)?
These types of beatings are strikes by objects that break the skin. Examples include baseball bats, planks of wood, clubs, crowbars, tire irons, rakes, axes, shovels, chairs, or just about anything else you can imagine. Once the initial strike breaks the skin, blood is thrown out from the injury and produces a medium velocity impact spatter pattern. That same blow will

cover the weapon with blood. The next swing (backward and then forward again) creates a cast-off pattern on the wall or ceiling. Every strike creates a new medium velocity impact spatter pattern and recovers the instrument with fresh blood, which allows for another cast-off line if it is swung again. Investigators count the number of cast-off patterns (adding one more for the initial blow) to obtain a fairly accurate estimate of how many times the victim was hit.

The medium velocity impact spatter patterns can be evaluated for Point of Origin determinations, identifying where each wound was positioned within the room.

These wounds create significant bleeding, so you should consider whether there was enough blood to drip and enough blood to leave prints when answering the questions below.

Is There A Cutting?

Cuts and slices can occur from almost any sharp weapon: knives, swords, box cutters, broken glass, claws. Cuts act under the same principles as the blunt force of a beating, but there are some differences of note. Because these items are sharp, the skin does not act as sufficiently as a barrier as with blunt force traumas. In those cases, the force (and therefore most of the injury) was at the surface, while with sharp objects, the force can continue inward, making the injury deeper. Since the injuries of cuttings are more internal, there is less chance of producing a medium velocity impact spatter pattern from the injury site. However, just like with a beating, cast-off patterns are still created after each swing once an injury has been made (with no cast-offs from the first swing).

Because a knife tends to have less surface area than a club, less blood transfers to the weapon. This means the cast-off patterns have fewer blood dot stains and the line may be more subtle than one created during a beating. Nevertheless, investigators can still identify the patterns, and make an accurate estimate of how many times the victim was cut.

Because lacerations in the skin tend to go deeper than a blunt force injury, they bleed much easier. Consider the area injured and the angle of attack. The site of the incision will determine the volume of blood in the scene; an arterial spray creates a very different pattern than other cuts. If your victim is cut, you should definitely consider having drip patterns in the scene as well as possible bloody prints.

> **PITFALL** – Dead bodies don't bleed! A postmortem (after death) stab wound is very different from a living person's wound. The heart stops at death and blood is no longer moving through the body. Livor mortis begins, which is the blood draining out of its vessels down to the gravity dependent area of the body (the part of the body on the ground). Medical Examiners can distinguish between antemortem (before death) and postmortem wounds. So if someone is going to keep stabbing a victim after he is dead, although there could still be some blood, it's not going to be in the same volume as the antemortem stabs, and therefore not produce the same clear bloodstain patterns.

Is There Enough Blood To Drip?

Drips happen when there is enough blood at an elevated surface (such as from an injury on a victim) that gravity is able to pull off individual drops. An active wound will leave several drips as the bleeding continually replenishes the blood. The drops fall at a 90-degree angle and create circular low velocity impact stains on the ground. If the surface a drip lands on, however, is rough, the circular stain is disrupted and can leave a very irregular shape.

If the person who is bleeding is able to move around the scene, either during the course of the altercation or after, the bleeder will leave a drip stain path behind him. Investigators can later follow this trail of blood drops and map the person's movement.

Remember, if you're having a character bleed sig-

internal, there is less chance of producing a medium velocity impact spatter pattern from the injury site. However, just like with a beating, cast-off patterns are still created after each swing once an injury has been made (with no cast-offs from the first swing).

Because a knife tends to have less surface area than a club, less blood transfers to the weapon. This means the cast-off patterns have fewer blood dot stains and the line may be more subtle than one created during a beating. Nevertheless, investigators can still identify the patterns, and make an accurate estimate of how many times the victim was cut.

Because lacerations in the skin tend to go deeper than a blunt force injury, they bleed much easier. Consider the area injured and the angle of attack. The site of the incision will determine the volume of blood in the scene; an arterial spray creates a very different pattern than other cuts. If your victim is cut, you should definitely consider having drip patterns in the scene as well as possible bloody prints.

> **PITFALL** – Dead bodies don't bleed! A postmortem (after death) stab wound is very different from a living person's wound. The heart stops at death and blood is no longer moving through the body. Livor mortis begins, which is the blood draining out of its vessels down to the gravity dependent area of the body (the part of the body on the ground). Medical Examiners can distinguish between antemortem (before death) and postmortem wounds. So if someone is going to keep stabbing a victim after he is dead, although there could still be some blood, it's not going to be in the same volume as the antemortem stabs, and therefore not produce the same clear bloodstain patterns.

Is There Enough Blood To Drip?

Drips happen when there is enough blood at an elevated surface (such as from an injury on a victim) that gravity is able to pull off individual drops. An active wound will leave several drips as the bleeding continually replenishes the blood. The drops fall at a 90-degree angle and create circular low velocity impact stains on the ground. If the surface a drip lands on, however, is rough, the circular stain is disrupted and can leave a very irregular shape.

If the person who is bleeding is able to move around the scene, either during the course of the altercation or after, the bleeder will leave a drip stain path behind him. Investigators can later follow this trail of blood drops and map the person's movement.

Remember, if you're having a character bleed significantly, each person only has about a gallon of blood. A gallon can be stretched pretty far, but it won't fill a bathtub.

If the blood drips are from a stationary object, such as blood dripping off of a baseball bat hanging over the edge of a table, the drips will all fall from the same area and therefore hit the same spot on the ground. This drip-into-drip action produces several spines and satellites around the main bloodstain.

Drip stains also provide the opportunity for other bloodstain patterns in your scene. Drips are often easy to overlook, and can be walked through or smeared in hasty clean-up attempts. This can leave ring stains or wipes, as addressed below in the section on clean-up attempts.

Is There Enough Blood To Leave Prints?

Depending on the type and severity of the wounds, a victim can bleed significantly within a scene. Is there enough blood in your altercation for it to be transferred to another place? Contact patterns occur when a bloody object leaves an impression of itself on a non-bloody surface.

A victim grasping a significant injury can leave a bloody handprint behind if he reached for the wall for balance. A shoeprint can reveal the size or type of shoe if someone walked through a blood puddle. Any object with enough blood on it will leave behind its bloody imprint if placed on a non-bloody surface.

Also, if there is blood on someone's clothing or hand (or fur!), that person/animal can leave swipes on walls, doors and any other surface if that blood is brushed up against it. Investigators use swipes to tell which direction the bloody person was moving in.

Are There Objects In The Way Of The Blood's Path?

What is in the scene where the injury occurs? What's the layout? What's between the victim and the surface the blood is sprayed on? If an object gets in the way of the blood's trajectory, you need to consider having a void pattern in your scene. This occurs when something stops some of the blood from reaching the same surface as the rest of the blood. Void patterns are often "shadows" of the intermediary object. Investigators can use the void pattern to identify what the object was.

If the object is still in its position when the CSIs arrive, the void pattern should not affect the investigation to any degree. However, if that object is missing, investigators now have to determine what it was and why it was important enough to take away.

Is There A Clean-Up Attempt?

In many scenes, the suspect attempts to do a quick cleaning to make sure there is nothing that leads the police to him/her. Often times, this clean-up is hastily done and is ineffective.

Many clean-up attempts leave behind blood ring stains. The surface tension of a blood drip tries to form that liquid into a sphere, even when on the ground. As a result, most of the blood in that stain is pulled to the center of it. Having the least amount of blood at the edges of the stain means the outer ring dries first. When there is a quick clean-up attempt, with no time for scrubbing, the inside, liquid, part of the stain is wiped away, but the dried outer ring remains behind. These rings always mean the scene has been altered. Most claims of suicide or acting in self-defense are easily debunked if cleaning can be proven.

Also, a cleaning attempt can leave wipe marks from wet stains. A wipe is a stroke made from blood already on the surface.

Are There Any Complicating Factors?

Do you need to make things difficult for your investigators? Should your scene not be as cut-and-dried as the experts promise? There are several things you can do as an author to make the bloodstain patterns more complicated.

If the scene is intense in its nature, meaning that multiple injuries occurred, overlapping bloodstain patterns could prove to be confusing or altered. A good bloodstain pattern analyst needs to take her time to identify every possible stain over the same area. It is time consuming and difficult to differentiate, but essential for an accurate crime reconstruction.

Animal activity is a very real problem in crime scene processing. If a pet is active within a bloody scene before it is discovered, or if the scene is outdoors and open to wildlife, animal involvement can alter the scene.

Animals can walk through pools of blood and leave paw prints over other vital evidence such as drip stains. They can lie in blood and get their fur coated in it. Then they may leave blood marks (mostly swipes) throughout the scene that could be misleading to the investigators. They can also leave the impression a clean-up was attempted if their fur wipes up existing stains.

Intentional misdirection is also a possibility. If the culprit is savvy enough, he may create additional bloodstain patterns to confuse investigators (by creating his own drip patterns or splashing in existing blood). Perhaps he will attempt to stage the scene so the investigators come to the wrong conclusion. He could put the knife in the victim's hand, or hang the body in attempts to suggest suicide. He could also attempt to clean the scene so the investigators have no idea what happened.

Writing Examples

Now that we've set up the questions as a map to what the bloodstain patterns should look like in your scene, let's go through some examples of how the questions lead to the actual storytelling.

Remember, blood does not have to be the central focus of your story. In a murder mystery or gory tale, blood takes a big role, but in some stories the blood may only be present for one chapter, adding depth to a story without overtaking it. I'm going to give some examples from a variety of genres.

Contemporary Mystery

> SPATTER MENU –
> Gunshot? Yes   Beating/Hand? No
> Beating/Instrument? No   Cutting? No
> Drips? No   Prints? No
> Voids? No   Clean-Up? Yes (Shooter hands)
> Complications? Yes (initial story)

911 received a desperate call from Kimberly, who reported her best friend, Robin, just called her to say she was going to commit suicide. Kimberly was on her way but wanted to see if the cops could get there faster and attempt to stop her. First responders gained access to Robin's apartment and found Robin's body in the living room, shot in the head. The gun was nearby, and about two and a half feet above the floor on the wall closest to Robin's body was a circular pattern of blood.

The individual droplets that made up the pattern were so small it appeared the wall was stained pink within the pattern. The detective correctly identified this as a misting pattern and was initially satisfied with Kimberly's story that Robin committed suicide. Kimberly eventually showed up to the apartment and agreed to be interviewed and provide the detective with anything he needed. Something about Kimberly's demeanor bothered the detective, but he couldn't put his finger on what.

Days later, upon reevaluating the scene photos, the detective noted both of Robin's hands were clean. He knew that a gunshot wound produces back spatter, which should have been present on Robin's hand.

The detective pieced together that there was no way Robin's shooting hand could have avoided the blowback spatter because she would have had no choice but to shoot herself at pointblank range. He knew it was ridiculous to consider Robin could have somehow gotten up, washed her hand and then come back to the spot she shot herself. The only scenario that made sense was someone else had shot her.

Since this was not self-inflicted, then the story that Robin was going to commit suicide became immediately suspect, and the person telling that tale was Kimberly. The detective called Kimberly into the station under the pretense of a re-interview. He knew there would be no chance of any evidence of her involvement from her hands, as too many days had passed. He also realized chances were that any clothing Kimberly wore would also have been cleaned. During the interview, Kimberly, as eager to cooperate as before, consented to a search of her car and home.

These searches provided three pieces of blood evidence linking Kimberly to the scene. The brake pedal had traces of blood on it, a pair of white sneakers had minute blood drops around the laces, and a jacket had dried blood on an inner sleeve. In her rush to clean up and get back to the scene on the day of the shooting, Kimberly did not think to clean these items. The blood came back as Robin's and Kimberly was arrested.

By the time her trial date arrived, the detective managed to procure two other significant pieces of evidence against her.

First, the Medical Examiner at autopsy found that the entrance wound was at the back of Robin's head, the exit wound at her forehead. No one committing suicide puts the gun at the back of her head, it's too awkward. Second, Kimberly's cell phone pings placed her much closer to Robin's apartment than she claimed to be when she called 911.

In this story, Kimberly shot Robin in the back of the head after she had Robin kneel facing away from her. The misting pattern on the wall fit the injury, which is the accuracy you as writers are striving for. The key to solving this case was the *missing* blood on

Robin's hands. Often, where blood isn't turns out to be as important as where it is.

Contemporary Thriller

SPATTER MENU –	
Gunshot? Yes	Beating/Hand? No
Beating/Instrument? No	Cutting? No
Drips? Yes	Prints? Yes
Voids? No	Clean-Up? Yes (Shooter hands)
Complications? Yes (Story/Weapon)	

Tere, a CIA operative, was on assignment to recruit Michael, an official for the Saudi Arabian government and suspected spy. At 3:30 AM, Tere called her security task force to the operational safe house and reported she had shot Michael. She claimed he had been attacking her.

Tere's handler, Elle, must now carefully spin a delicate web that explains Michael's death and keeps the fragile relationship between the countries intact while also probing into Tere's story. The US government wants Tere out of the country, the Saudi government wants explanations and Elle has no time to piece together what really happened.

When the security detail arrived at the safe house, they found Michael's body just inside Tere's room with a bullet wound to the head. A thorough search revealed blood in a misting pattern at about Michael's height on the door frame and out into the hall.

Downstairs they found blood in the bathroom sink and then passive drips of blood from the bathroom to the kitchen. Several more drips were by the back sliding glass door. They also found swipe marks on the door's handle and on one of the drawers.

When asked for her account, Tere stated she had been out with Michael having drinks, attempting to find her "in" with him, when he began hitting on her. She said she teased him just enough to make him want to come back for more before saying good night and making her way to the safe house.

Tere claimed a few hours later someone broke into the house and forced himself into her room. She said he attacked her with a knife from the kitchen. She claimed she shot him in self-defense, called her security team from her cell phone and stayed in her bed collecting herself until they arrived. It wasn't until she stepped over the body to let the security team in that she realized the trespasser was Michael.

When she answered the door, she presented the team with a knife. She showed them a few minor cuts on her abdomen and a nastier gash on her inner left arm.

Elle had a nagging doubt about Tere's account, but it wasn't until she considered the blood spatter patterns that she began to prove Tere was lying.

First, there was no blood on or near the bed where Tere claimed to have been during and after the incident. Michael's body and the spatter on the door indicated Michael was there when he was shot, not at the bed cutting Tere. The knife Tere presented to the police showed no discernible blood on the blade. The only other blood in the house was downstairs, away from the bedroom, although Tere claimed she did not leave her room. A significant number of passive blood drips were found at the back door, along with a swipe. Upon searching behind the house, security found a bloody ice pick.

Elle races time and proves the actual story, which is supported by the bloodstain patterns. Tere was also working for the Saudi government as a double-agent for a price, but sold them bogus information. Michael was assigned to expose her. Once she realized Michael's true goal, Tere invited him back to the safe house. Tere went upstairs and eventually called Michael up to her room. Michael most likely went willingly, but was not expecting when he opened the door Tere would shoot him.

Panicked about making it seem like a justifiable killing, Tere created a self-defense story. She ran downstairs and grabbed an ice pick from the kitchen. She went to the downstairs bathroom, where she attempted to slash her abdomen, but only really made the slightest of cuts, and then stuck the ice pick in her inner left arm, not realizing that a defensive wound should be on the outside of the arm. Self-inflicted wounds are on the inner arms.

Anticipating the arrival of security, she went back to the kitchen, leaving a trail of blood drops behind her and threw the ice pick out the back door. The blood swipe was created when she opened the door. Too late, she realized she would need to provide a weapon if she claimed Michael was attacking her, so went back into the kitchen and opened the utensil drawer to get a knife, marking the drawer with her blood as well.

The scene will always tell the story if it's allowed to, so when writing a scene, it has to be consistent with the actual events, even if the characters are attempting to cover it up.

Historical Romance

SPATTER MENU –	
Gunshot? No	Beating/Hand? No
Beating/Instrument? No	Cutting? Yes
Drips? No	Prints? No
Voids? No	Clean-Up? No
Complications? Yes (Lack of Blood)	

This story is a Victorian romance between Police Constable Benjamin Stein and a prostitute he saves from Jack the Ripper. He becomes involved with the case after the murder of the first victim, Polly Nichols, who was found outside of a stable near Whitechapel in 1888.

Pedestrians found Nichols with stab wounds to her abdomen and her throat slashed. Because of what appeared to be a lack of blood (which was actually absorbed by her clothing), initial investigators believed she was killed elsewhere and dumped at this scene.

To make a police constable a believable part of the entire Jack the Ripper investigation, you could make Stein instrumental at this first scene by being the one to determine this was indeed the site of the murder. You could have him correctly identify the arterial spurt pattern on the stable wall, which could not have happened if Nichols was already dead.

Likewise, if he realized that the blood had been absorbed by the clothing, it could lead him to the place Nichols stole her dress, and to its original owner, the feisty prostitute who will become his love interest.

Paranormal Thriller

> **SPATTER MENU –**
> Gunshot? Yes
> Beating/Hand? No
> Beating/Instrument? No
> Cutting? Yes (Claws)
> Drips? Yes
> Prints? Yes
> Voids? No
> Clean-Up? No
> Complications? Yes (Paranormal)

The heroine for this story, Pamela, comes from a rare clan of shifter hunters, and is an expert tracker and fighter. After several recent murders, she believes the shifter hunters were being hunted themselves.

On the night of this killing, she arrived at the

bloody cabin after the cops had already starting processing the scene. Her federal pass got her inside. She soon realized this is the bloodiest scene yet.

As with the other murders, the body was gone. Three walls showed distinct misting patterns. Pamela smiled. Her fellow hunter had fought back, shooting the shifter several times with a shotgun.

Cast-off patterns covered every surface, consistent with the claw marks at the front door. One window was open and the frame showed smears of bloody streaks…swipe marks, probably from bloody fur. The shifter hadn't reverted before fleeing with the body. The pools of blood on the floor indicated that one of them had been bleeding badly, which meant Pamela could track them.

The local sheriff didn't believe in the paranormal and told Pamela without that federal pass, he'd throw her butt out of the county. Pamela grinned and asked the sheriff how high the ceiling was inside the cabin. The sheriff responded, "Probably twelve feet, why?"

Pamela suggested the sheriff order a bloodstain pattern analysis and left the cabin headed towards the woods, towards her mark.

The sheriff was completely dumbfounded after the bloodstain pattern analysis revealed many of the patterns had Points of Origin at nine feet in the air…

Spatter Chart

Below is a structured chart I put together to illustrate

what weapons and actions create which bloodstains. Consult the below chart if you need help determining what type of bloodstain would result from which specific action, or conversely, if you want a certain bloodstain pattern, what needs to happen to create it. The intention is to provide a quick reference to use when putting all of the pieces together.

PATTERN TYPE	SPATTER TYPE	SPATTER SPECIFICS	CAUSE OF SPATTER	EXTRA NOTES
High Velocity Impact Spatter	Misting	Forward Spatter	Gunshot Wound	
High Velocity Impact Spatter	Misting	Forward Spatter	Explosion	
High Velocity Impact Spatter	Blowback	Back Spatter	Entrance Wound	Blowback can Land on Shooter
Medium Velocity Impact Spatter	Cast-Off	Overhead and/or on Walls	Beating with Bat/Club/Axe/Pipe	Minus the First, Each Swing Creates a New Cast-Off Pattern.
Medium Velocity Impact Spatter	Cast-Off	Overhead and/or on Walls	Stabbing with Knife	- Bludgeon's Pattern Pronounced
Medium Velocity Impact Spatter	Cast-Off	Horizontal on Walls	Cutting/Slicing with Knife	- Knife's Less Obvious Due to Fewer Drips in Pattern
Medium Velocity Impact Spatter	Arterial Spurts	Arched Patterns	Artery Must Be Cut	
Low Velocity Impact Spatter	Misting	Expirated Blood	Blood Breathed Out from Lungs as Mist	Always Near Face
Low Velocity Impact Spatter	Passive Drips	90-Degree Circular Stain	Active Wound or Enough Blood to Drip (Theirs or Another's)	
Post-Impact Stains	Flow Pattern	Gravity Pulls Blood in Finger Streams to Lowest Point		
Miscellaneous	Void Pattern	Blood Not Where It Should Be	Blood Strikes an Intermediary Surface	
Altered Stains	Swipe	Feathered in Direction of Travel	Blood Brushed onto Clean Surface	Blood Can Be Left by Bloody Hand, Clothing or Pet Fur
Altered Stains	Wipe	Feathered in Direction of Travel	Blood Already on Surface is Smeared	Seen Often in Clean-Up Attempts
Altered Stains	Contact Pattern	Bloodstain Takes the Shape of Bloody Object	Bloody Object Leaves Blood on Surface	Bloody Handprints, Shoeprints, & Weapon Shapes Identifiable

Figure 34: Spatter Chart

Closing Thoughts

> "Yet who would have thought the old man to have had so much blood in him."
> *Macbeth* by William Shakespeare

You now have all the tools at your disposal to make your stories bloody brilliant! There is a lot of material, but it can all be summed up pretty easily.

- Blood follows simple physics rules.
- The amount of force behind the injury creates one of three types of impact spatters: Low velocity, Medium velocity and High velocity.
- Patterns are mostly Spatter Stains, Altered Stains or Passive Stains.
- Bloodstains can tell the directionality of the blood drop, which can lead to an Area of Convergence estimation and a Point of Origin calculation.

As you're writing your scene, don't forget to go through the Spatter Menu questions above to verify every pattern that should be in your scene is covered.

And finally, as with every forensic topic I teach, let me remind you how important it is to *solve your crime before you commit it to paper*! Knowing how your protagonist resolves everything will only aid you in adding complications earlier in the story. Having to make up a solution at the last minute is an easy way to torpedo all of the work you put into the book previously.

Three is no reason to be nervous when it comes to including blood, no matter what story you're writing. With all you now know about spatters, go out and "leave a mark" on your genre!

Glossary

Altered Stains – A category of bloodstains that occur after the incident that caused the original bloodstain patterns in the scene. They can be bloodstains that were changed or be new stains added after the fact, such as swipes, wipes or contact patterns.

Angle of Impact – The acute angle at which a blood droplet strikes a surface, whether that surface is horizontal or vertical.

Animal Activity – Altered stains caused by animals. Examples include paw prints, fur swipes or stains caused by insect activity active in the scene.

Antemortem – A Latin term used in medicine and forensics meaning prior to death.

Arc Sine – An inverse trigonometric function that determines an angle from any of that angle's trigonometric ratios. In blood spatter analysis, the arc sine is used to determine the angle of impact for an individual bloodstain using the stain's width and length.

Area of Convergence – The intersecting area, on a two-dimensional surface, created by determining the directionality of several blood droplets, that indicates the area the blood originated from.

Arterial Spurts – An arched bloodstain pattern created from blood exiting the body from a severed artery. The arched pattern corresponds to the heartbeats, which provides the pressure to expel the blood.

Back Spatter – Blood that is directed back toward the source of the force that caused the injury. In gunshots, it is from the entrance wound, and only travels a few feet. Also, **Blowback**.

Blood Drop – A volume of blood (typically 0.05 mL) that gravity is able to pull from the parent source of blood by exceeding the surface tension. Drops are spherical, not a teardrop shape. A series of blood drops created by the same injury-inducing incident create a bloodstain pattern. Also, **Droplet**.

Blood Spatter – Bloodstain patterns created by several droplets when a force is introduced to a blood source. The patterns produced are often characteristic of the nature of the forces that created them.

Blood Spatter Analysis – The systematic procedure of analyzing bloodstain patterns to reconstruct the crime. Also, **Bloodstain Pattern Analysis**.

Bloodborne Pathogens – Diseases caused by exposure to blood, or sometimes other body fluids. Hepatitis B (HBV), Hepatitis C (HCV) and the Human Immunodeficiency Virus (HIV) are examples of bloodborne pathogens.

Bloodstain – The shapes blood makes once it reaches a surface. It can be a pool, a flow pattern, a contact pattern or as small as a single microscopic blood droplet.

Bloodstain Pattern – The overall look blood forms from several bloodstains made from a single event.

Bloodstain Pattern Analysis – An acceptable synonym for **Blood Spatter Analysis**.

Blowback – In bloodstain pattern analysis, an acceptable synonym for **Back Spatter**.

Cast-Off Marks – Additional blood shapes formed when blood was thrown out from the main stain at impact. These marks are not considered for any analysis beyond general directionality. Cast-off marks are either **Spines** or **Satellite Stains**.

Cast-Off Patterns – A type of spatter stain caused by blood drops projected off a blood covered object via centrifugal or inertial forces. The pattern results in a line of drops. The number of lines indicates how many blows were made with the object, but you must add one more blow to the total as the object was not covered in blood for the first strike.

Centrifugal Force – This is the force created by an object traveling in a circular or arced path. It is a force projecting away from the path. It is this force that is responsible for creating many of the Cast-Off patterns found when an object covered in blood is swung.

Close-Up Shot – A photograph taken at extreme close range that only captures the evidence of interest. In blood spatter, it is only of the spatter pattern, or perhaps of an individual blood drop stain, without anything else in the picture.

Contact Pattern – A bloodstain pattern created when a bloody object comes into contact with a non-blood surface. The pattern often takes the shape of the object.

Crime Scene Investigators – Law enforcement officials specially trained in overall or specific evidence collection at crime scenes.

Crime Scene Kit – A duffle bag or bin of necessary items used by a responding law enforcement official at crime scenes. The requirements for kits can vary from agency to agency, but typically contain evidence collection materials (bags, jars, labels, markers), flashlights, pens, pads of paper, agency forms and Personal Protective Equipment. For bloodstain pattern analysts, kits also include a ball of string, a protractor and a scientific calculator (or arc sine charts).

CSIs – Crime Scene Investigators.

Directionality – Determining what path the blood drop was traveling on. To find the origin of the blood, you take the opposite bearing.

Drip Patterns – A passive bloodstain pattern in which gravity causes blood drops to fall from the parent blood source. Each drip falls into the surface pattern, creating spines and satellite patterns. An acceptable synonym for **Satellite Staining**.

Droplet – In bloodstain pattern analysis, an acceptable synonym for **Blood Drop.**

Expirated Bloodstain Patterns – Blood that has entered a person's airway system and is breathed out as a bloody mist. The resulting pattern is similar to a high velocity impact spatter pattern, but is only found near and on the person's face.

Feathering – In bloodstain patters, a tapering effect as blood is moved across a non-bloody surface, often found in swipes and wipes. The feathering always points in the direction the blood was brushed towards.

Finger Flow Patterns – In bloodstain patterns, the individual streams of blood gravity pulls in a passive flow pattern.

First Responders – An emergency service unit sent to answer an urgent distress call. First responders are made up of the police, firefighters and Emergency Medical Technicians (EMTs). The first responsibility is the protection of life and property, followed by the preservation of the scene for the arrival of investigators.

Flow Patterns – A bloodstain that has been altered by gravity, pulling the blood down to the lowest point.

Force – A strength/energy exerted upon an object. In blood spatter analysis, it is what caused the injury and expelled the blood. The power of the force determines the size of the blood drops and the level of impact spatter pattern that is created.

Forward Spatter – Blood that is thrown along with the force creating the injury. In gunshots, it is from the exit wound.

Free Fall – A situation in which the only force acting upon a falling object is gravity. In blood spatter analysis it is a **Passive Drip**.

High Velocity Impact Spatter – Bloodstains created from an extreme force, typically found in gunshot wounds and explosions. The droplets in these stains are incredibly tiny and create a "misting" look in the resulting stain. The force from this type of blow typically creates two injury sites: the entrance wound and the exit wound, creating both forward spatter and back spatter.

Impact Patterns – A type of spatter stain that originates from the injury itself, as opposed from being flung from an intermediate object.

Inertia – The propensity of an item to maintain its current state of movement. Blood traveling on an object that suddenly stops will keep moving, being flung off the object via its inertia.

Kiesselbach's Plexus – A region of the nasal septum where multiple blood vessels converge, including four arteries. This is the region that most nosebleeds occur from and is why the bleeding is so difficult to stop. The area was named for Wilhelm Kiesselbach, a German Ear/Nose/Throat doctor.

Livor Mortis – The staining of the skin as the blood in the body pools in the gravity-dependent areas based on its position. Once the heart stops beating at death, the blood begins to leak out of the cardiovascular vessels. It eventually stains the skin where it settles in a bluish-purple discoloration.

Low Velocity Impact Spatter – Passive bloodstains created by the force of gravity.

Medium Velocity Impact Spatter – Bloodstains created by a force greater than gravity, creating smaller blood droplets than those found in low velocity impact spatters. Cast-Off patterns are a common type of medium velocity impact spatter found in beatings and stabbings.

Mid-Range Shot – A photograph taken to show the evidence of interest and its position in the room as well its proximity to close by items. It is a shot from which the evidence can be identified, but is not focused only on the evidence.

Misting – A bloodstain pattern in which the individual droplets are so small and plentiful that the surface on which they landed appears to be stained pink. Misting can occur in one of two circumstances: By a high velocity impact spatter injury or by an actual mist that is breathed out in an expired bloodstain.

Origin – The place where the bloodstain came from. Also, **Source**.

Overall Shot – A photograph taken to show as much of the environment around the evidence of interest as possible. If indoors it could be an entire room taken from the doorway. If outdoors, it's as wide a shot as possible. The evidence may not necessarily be identified in this shot, but it establishes the entire surroundings of the evidence.

Parent Drop/Parent Pool – The main bloodstain that caused secondary bloodstains such as spines, satellites or finger flow patterns.

Passive Bloodstains – A category of bloodstains that occur because of gravity or other environment factor, independent of the blood-inducing incident. Also, **Passive Drip**.

Passive Drip – In bloodstain pattern analysis, an acceptable synonym for **Passive Bloodstains**.

Passive Force – A constant, consistent force which is applied naturally without any human involvement. In bloodstain pattern analysis it is another name for gravity, and produces low velocity impact spatter patterns.

Pattern Transfer – In bloodstain pattern analysis, an acceptable synonym for **Contact Pattern**.

Personal Protective Equipment – Any of a variety of

outer layer disposable clothing intended to create a barrier between potential pathogens and the person working in or around blood or other possible contagions. Appropriate PPE can be any or all of the following: latex gloves, shoe booties, sleeves, goggles, aprons, masks and full bio-hazard suits.

Point of Origin – The intersecting area, in three-dimensional space, that pinpoints exactly where the bloodstain originated from. This is determined by calculating the angle of impact for several blood drops within the bloodstain pattern and stringing the path followed based on that angle. Where the strings intersect is the point of origin; that is, where the injury-causing incident occurred.

Postmortem – A Latin term used in medicine and forensics meaning after death.

PPE – Personal Protective Equipment.

Satellite Staining – In bloodstain pattern analysis, an acceptable synonym for **Drip Patterns**.

Satellite Stains – A ring of tiny individual droplets that create a ring around the parent blood drop.

Source – In bloodstain pattern analysis, an acceptable synonym for **Origin**.

Spatter Stains – A category of bloodstains that

requires a force greater than gravity and is indicative violence has occurred.

Specialist – An expert trained in a specific field. In blood spatter analysis, it is an investigator specifically trained in bloodstain pattern analysis.

Spine – A small cast-off droplet from a parent drop that creates a trunk extending from the parent drop.

Surface – The outer most layer of an object, such as a floor, wall or ceiling.

Surface Tension – The force that exists in liquids that keeps them together. For a drop or splash to separate from the liquid, another force must be present that can overcome the surface tension. Surface tension is what makes liquids form spheres when in the air.

Swipe – A type of Altered Stain where blood is transferred onto a clean surface by a bloody item, such as a bloody hand, sleeve, fur or other object.

Terminal Velocity – The velocity reached when the air resistance pushing against a falling object reaches the same level as the force of gravity pulling the object. At this point, the object will not fall any faster.

Trajectory – The path taken by an object moving in air or space while influenced by forces. In blood spatter analysis, it is the route taken by a blood drop from injury to stain.

Viscosity – The force within a liquid that works against its propensity to flow. Honey has a much higher viscosity than water does. Blood's viscosity is comparable to that of whole milk.

Void Patterns – Clean areas within a bloody scene that logic would dictate should have blood, but none is present. These are created by objects that were in the way of the blood's path which intercepted the blood before it could hit the surface with the rest of the blood, creating a clean area of the object's "shadow." Often times the item's size and shape can be determined by the void pattern.

Wipe – A type of Altered Stain where a clean object brushes existing blood on a surface across the surface. The difference between a wipe and a swipe is in a wipe the blood is already present, it's just pushed around, while a swipe occurs on a clean surface.

Bibliography

- *Bloodstain Pattern Analysis with an Introduction to Crime Scene Reconstruction, (3rd Edition)* by Tom Bevel and Ross M. Gardner, (2008)
- *Scientific and Legal Applications of Bloodstain Pattern Interpretation* by Stuart H. James, (1998)
- *Principles of Bloodstain Pattern Analysis: Theory and Practice* by Stuart H. James and Paul E. Kish, (2005)
- *Crime Investigation* by Dr. Paul Leland Kirk, (1953)
- *Henry Lee's Crime Scene Handbook* by Henry C. Lee and Timothy Palmbach, (2001)
- *Bloodstain Pattern Interpretation* by Herbert MacDonell, (1982)
- *Flight Characteristics and Stain Patterns of Human Blood* by Herbert MacDonell, (1971)
- *Criminalistics: An Introduction to Forensic Science (10th Edition)* by Richard Saferstein, (2010)
- *Human Anatomy (5th Edition)* by Kenneth Saladin, (2016)

Index

A

ACCURACY, 4, 5, 7, 10, 56, 62, 68, 80, 91
Altered Stains, 49, 50, 54, 55, 133, 135, 145, 146
Angle of Impact, 16, 17, 18, 19, 20, 21, 22, 56, 83, 85, 86, 87, 88, 135, 144
Animal Activity, 55, 92, 122, 135
Arc Sine, 88, 135, 139
Area of Convergence, 84, 85, 86, 99, 133, 136
Arterial Spurts, 48, 81, 111, 136

B

Back Spatter/Blowback, 40, 80, 81, 90, 113, 114, 136, 137
Beatings, 7, 38, 39, 46, 75, 79, 90, 114, 115, 142
Blood Pressure, 47
Blood Rings, 54, 55, 81, 119, 121
Blood Spatter Analysis, 3, 4, 5, 10, 11, 35, 66, 68, 82, 86, 91, 92, 135, 136
Blood, Volume in a Body, 11, 12, 110, 119
Bloodborne Pathogens, 66, 67, 137, 144
Bloodstain Pattern Analysis, 3, 4, 20, 63, 72, 85, 89, 91, 137

C

Case Studies, 27, 101
Cast-off Marks, 19, 22, 23, 42, 43, 137
Cast-off Patterns, 41, 42, 43, 44, 46, 75, 76, 77, 78, 79, 97, 116, 117, 137, 138
Centrifugal Force, 43, 46, 97, 137, 138
Clean-up Attempts, 50, 54, 55, 69, 81, 119, 120, 121, 122
Close-up Shots (Photography), 70, 138
Contact Patterns, 50, 51, 81, 119, 135, 138
Crime Scene Kit, 66, 67, 82, 138
Crime Scene Photography, 69, 70, 71, 138, 142, 143
Cuttings, 78, 116, 117

D

Directionality, 15, 20, 21, 22, 23, 83, 84, 85, 133, 136, 137, 139
Drip Patterns, 56, 115, 117, 122, 139

E

Entrance Wound, 40, 49, 80, 113, 136, 141
Exit Wound, 40, 49, 80, 113, 114, 140, 141
Expirated Bloodstain Patterns, 48, 49, 79, 80, 139, 142

F

Feathering, 52, 54, 139
Finger Flow Patterns, 58, 59, 60, 73, 91, 97, 140, 143
Fluids, 9, 137
Forward Spatter, 40, 80, 140, 141
Free Fall, 16, 24, 29, 87, 140
FUN FACT, 6, 11, 67, 115

G

Gisler, Bob and Barbara Harris (Case Study), 101, 102, 103, 104, 105, 106, 107
Gravity, 13, 16, 17, 24, 29, 36, 37, 38, 56, 58, 59, 60, 73, 74, 91, 97, 98, 112, 118, 136, 139, 140, 142, 143, 145
Gunshot Wounds, 7, 39, 41, 49, 90, 113, 114, 136, 140, 141

H

Harris, Bret (Case Study), 101, 102, 103, 104, 105, 106, 107
High Velocity Impact Spatter, 39, 40, 41, 48, 49, 73, 79, 80, 90, 111, 113, 114, 141, 142

I

Impact Patterns, 36, 37, 41, 141
Inertia, 44, 45, 46, 47, 97, 137, 141

K

Kiesselbach's Plexus, 115, 141
Kirk, Paul Leland, 5, 147

L

Low Velocity Impact Spatter, 37, 38, 72, 73, 74, 90, 118, 142, 143

M

MacDonell, Herbert, 6, 147
Medium Velocity Impact Spatter, 38, 39, 40, 73, 74, 75, 76, 79, 96, 113, 114, 115, 116, 117, 142
Mid-Range Shot (Photography), 70, 142
Misting, 40, 41, 48, 73, 79, 80, 114, 139, 141, 142

N

North, Darrell (Case Study), 27, 28, 29, 30, 31, 32, 33

O

Outdoor Scenes, 89, 90, 91, 92, 122, 143
Overall Shot (Photography), 70, 143

P

Passive Drips, 14, 16, 19, 23, 38, 56, 73, 74, 75, 92, 112, 133, 139, 142, 143
Pattern Transfer, 50, 143
Personal Protective Equipment/PPE, 66, 67, 139, 143, 144
Photographs, 69, 70, 71, 138, 142, 143
PITFALLS, 47, 60, 110, 111, 112, 118
Point of Origin, 36, 83, 85, 86, 87, 89, 114, 116, 133, 144
Pope, Curtis (Case Study), 27, 30, 31, 32, 33
PROCEDURE, 17, 21, 23, 37, 55, 73, 75, 79, 84, 85, 92

Q

Qualifications, 63, 64

R

Ring Patterns, 54, 55, 81, 119, 121

S

Satellite Cast-offs, 22, 23, 42, 43, 56, 57, 88, 119, 139, 143, 144

Sheppard, Sam, 5, 6
Slicings, 78, 116
Spatter Chart, 131
Spatter Menu, 112, 113, 114, 115, 116, 118, 119, 120, 121
Spatter Stains, 35, 36, 40, 41, 42, 43, 48, 133, 144
Spines, 19, 20, 21, 22, 23, 42, 43, 56, 83, 88, 98, 119, 139, 143, 145
Surface Tension, 9, 13, 14, 24, 25, 37, 43, 45, 56, 87, 121, 145
Swipes, 51, 52, 53, 54, 55, 81, 92, 112, 120, 122, 135, 139, 145

T

Terminal Velocity, 23, 24, 145
TERMS, 3, 12, 13, 16, 43, 54, 66, 88
Training, 64
Trajectory, 16, 92, 120, 145

V

Viscosity, 9, 12, 146
Void Patterns, 60, 61, 81, 120, 146

W

Wipes, 53, 54, 55, 81, 119, 121, 122, 135, 139, 146

About the Author

Geoff Symon is a twenty-year Federal Forensic Investigator and Polygraph Examiner. His participation in high-profile cases includes the attacks on September 11, 2001, the War in Iraq, the Space Shuttle Columbia explosion, the 2002 bombings in Bali and the Chandra Levy investigation, among countless other cases.

He has direct, first-hand experience investigating cases including murder (of all types), suicide, arson, kidnapping, bombings, sexual assault, child exploitation, theft and financial crimes. He has specified and certified training in the collection and preservation of evidence, blood spatter analysis, autopsies and laboratory techniques.

He has taught undergraduate and graduate-level college courses in forensics, including Basic Forensics, Crime Scene Processing and Crimes Against Children at the George Washington University (DC) and Marymount University (MD).

You can find him at GeoffSymon.com, Geoff Symon on Facebook and @geoffsymon on Twitter.